Whitehead's Ontology

Whitehead's Ontology

By John W. Lango

State University of New York Press
Albany · 1972

Whitehead's Ontology

First Edition

Published by State University of New York Press,
Thurlow Terrace, Albany, New York 12201

Most of Section 6 appeared as "The Relatedness of Eternal Objects in Whitehead's *Process and Reality*", *Process Studies*, vol. 1, no. 2 (Summer 1971): 124–128. Most of Sections 7 and 8 together with portions of 4, 15, and 17 appeared in "Towards Clarifying Whitehead's Theory of Concrescence", *Transactions of the Charles S. Peirce Society*, vol. 7, no. 3 (Summer 1971): 150–167. Grateful acknowledgment is made to the editors for permission to reprint.

This book was completed with the aid of a Faculty Research Fellowship for the summer of 1970 from The Research Foundation of State University of New York.

Printed in the United States of America

Library of Congress Cataloging in Publication Data
Lango, John W
    Whitehead's ontology.
    Includes bibliographical references.
    1. Whitehead, Alfred North, 1861–1947.
Process and reality.   2. Ontology. I. Title.
B1674.W353P76   113   78-171184
ISBN 0-87395-093-3
ISBN 0-87395-193-X (microfiche)

To Carol

Contents

Preface

This book is an essay on the ontology implicit in the metaphysical system stated by Alfred North Whitehead in *Process and Reality*.[1] Its goal—defining the types of entity in his ontology (Chapter 3)—is essentially grounded upon a somewhat detailed interpretation of his metaphysical system (Chapter 2).

A peculiarity that sets it apart from most writings on *Process and Reality* is the use of logic—in particular, the logic of relations—to define the types of entity. This indicates that, even though Whitehead's career is often divided into periods, there is no hiatus between his later metaphysical speculation and his earlier writings in mathematics, logic, physics, and the philosophy of science. In short, this indicates that the Whitehead of *Principia Mathematica* is at work in *Process and Reality*.

My interpretation of his metaphysics primarily involves not an explication of the text of *Process and Reality* but rather an analysis of the system of categories stated in that text. In contrast to the customary emphasis on actual entities, eternal objects, and the relations of prehension and ingression, there are coequal discussions of the more neglected types of entity (e.g., contrasts) and relations between entities (e.g., concrescence). The purpose is to clarify sufficiently the internal coherence of his metaphysical system in order to ground adequately the definitions of the types of entity.

A more general purpose for writing this book has been to indicate that *Process and Reality* is not merely a milestone in the history of philosophy but a source of insights into contemporary problems.[2]

1

Introduction

1. *The Aim: Defining Whitehead's Categories of Existence*

Ontology is the study of being or beings. But what is being? Which are the beings? My aim is, in general, to understand the ontology implicit in the metaphysical system stated by Alfred North Whitehead in *Process and Reality*. I argue, in particular, that the beings of Whitehead's ontology are defined by the being.

The beings (entities) of an ontology are divisible into types (e.g., material bodies and minds). In Whitehead's ontology the types of entity are actual entities, prehensions, nexūs, subjective forms, eternal objects, propositions, multiplicities, and contrasts (the "Categories of Existence") (*PR* 32–33).[1] Ontological types, especially when so numerous, must be defined not haphazardly but through principles. I maintain, accordingly, that the types of entity in Whitehead's ontology are defined by a principle of being.

Being is the most universal "property" of entities. But does an entity have being simpliciter? I contend that, in Whitehead's ontology, being is, more appropriately, a relation between entities (which I term "synonty"). Thus his types of entity are defined by the principle that entities have being for one another (i.e., are synontic).

Entities are variously interrelated (e.g., by causality and by representation). Synonty, the most universal relation between entities, is also the most obscure. Relations more evident in Whitehead's metaphysics are, for example, prehension (which relates entities of all types to actual entities) and ingression (which relates eternal objects to actual entities). Therefore, in order to disclose the obscure but universal relation of synonty, I survey a variety of more evident special relations, most importantly, prehension, ingression, patterning, concrescence, mutual sensitivity, synthesis, and perception in the mode of presentational immediacy (Chapter 2).

Types of entity are partially understood (and might therefore be defined) through characteristic relations. For entities of each type have characteristic relations both to one another (e.g., material bodies causally interact) and to entities of other types (e.g., material bodies are represented in minds). Because the universal relation of synonty underlies special relations more evident in Whitehead's metaphysics, I define his types of entity simply by means of formal properties (from the logic of relations) of synonty (Chapter 3).

But Whitehead's metaphysics, because of the abstractness of its concepts, the richness of its themes, and the intricacy of its expression, is difficult to understand.[2] In particular, types of entity and relations between entities are perplexingly abundant. Therefore, as a preliminary to disclosing the universal relation of synonty and defining his types of entity, I consider some methods for understanding his metaphysics (Section 2).

In summary, my aim is to define Whitehead's types of entity (the "Categories of Existence") by means of formal properties of the universal relation of synonty.

2. *Some Methods for Understanding Whitehead's Metaphysics*

The "categories" (i.e., principles) of Whitehead's metaphysics (*PR* 30–42) may be understood most generally through generic philosophical concepts. For example, one of the "Categories of Existence" is the category of "Actual Entities" (*PR* 32). The meaning of this category may be adumbrated by the use of concepts such as "fundamental" and "derived": actual entities are the fundamental entities of his ontology because entities of all other types are derived from them.

Since generic philosophical concepts are learned through acquaintance with many philosophers' ideas, direct comparisons with other philosophers' metaphysics should be used for greater specification (*PR* v–vi). For instance, actual entities are like Leibniz's "monads" in that they are "mental", without "substantial" parts, "mirror" the universe, etc., but unlike them in that they "have windows", are temporal as well as spatial "atoms", are "physical" and not merely a "reality" "underlying" the physical, etc.

If only generic philosophical concepts and comparisons with other metaphysics are used, only a provisional understanding is achieved; it is necessary, as well, to elaborate Whitehead's metaphysics internally, by exploring the meaning of each category through its interconnections with the meanings of the other categories. For example, an actual entity is a subject aimed at in an internal process involving the concrescence of prehensions. The concepts of "subject", "(subjective) aim", "internal process of concrescence", and "prehension" are themselves the topics of other categories. Each of these concepts used to explain the nature of an actual entity may itself be understood through a similar mapping of its interconnections with other categories. For example, a prehension is a process of transition whereby antecedent actual entities enter into the self-immediacy of a concrescing actual entity. Also, the internal process of concrescence involves a succession of phases of prehensions with progressive elimination of indeterminateness resulting in the fully determinate satisfaction of the subject actual entity. In short, Whitehead's metaphysics must be understood through the internal coherence of its categories (*PR* 4–5, 9–10).

But Whitehead's metaphysics is also a theory about the world in which we live, a world "experienced" in a variety of ways—rudimentary (e.g., through sense-perception) and refined (e.g., through scientific theories). Hence his metaphysics must not only be coherent but must elucidate—and be elucidated by—the basic concepts and principles of each of the empirical theories which has been devised to account for the subject matter of these types of human experience (*PR* 4–6). For example, the "plenum" of spatio-temporally atomic actual entities is the basis for the four-dimensional space-time of the theory of relativity, and the web of those actual entities' prehensions of one another underlies the physicist's concept of "field".

Just as empirical theories are understood (and, of course, "tested") through observation and experiment, so a thorough understanding of a metaphysics requires the examination of particular instances illustrating its general categories. Comparisons with other metaphysics and elaborations of internal coherence involve a network of purely philosophical ideas; applications to empirical theories merely enlarge the network of ideas to include nonphilosophical ideas as well; but fuller understanding is only achieved when this circle of general concepts is transcended, and the instances which fall under these concepts are confronted. For example, the man Alfred North Whitehead is an instance of a society of actual entities (where societies comprise a type of nexus) (*PR* 50–52). More generally, each of the physical things which we observe with our senses is an instance of a society.

Examining instances may help to clarify the meaning of Whitehead's metaphysics, but it cannot account for the derivation of the concepts contained in that metaphysics. Metaphysical concepts, unlike colors, do not lie on the surface of things, waiting to be peeled off by the mind. Instead, their derivation is more subtle, and more circuitous: concepts which are ensconced in empirical theories, and thus which apply only to some things, are used metaphorically in metaphysics to apply to all (fundamental) things. This method of "imaginative generalization", used by Whitehead to derive his categories (*PR* 6–8), is of inestimable value in understanding them. For example, a human being experiences objects in his world. This concept of "experience", ordinarily applied only to humans (and perhaps to some other kinds of animal), is generalized by Whitehead to apply to all actual entities in the universe. But, since many of the peculiar features of human experiences, e.g., "consciousness", are not also features of the experiences of all actual entities, a more neutral term is chosen for this generalized concept of experience, namely, "prehension" (*PR* 37).

Although a metaphysics, derived by a process of speculation, is not to be asserted with dogmatic finality, but only to be entertained tentatively (*PR* 12), its principles should be stated with the "utmost precision and definiteness" (*PR* 13). There is no paradox here: the meaning must be clear, even though the truth is largely unknown. Therefore, although Whitehead states his metaphysics informally, there is good reason to "recast the scheme into a logical truth" (*PR* 13).[3] But there is another reason for applying logic to explicate the formal structure of his metaphysics, a reason which he does not expressly state: the complete generality of the metaphors, which are derived through imaginative generalization and tied together into a coherent system, is partly a generality expressible through the symbols of logic. For example, the metaphoric content of the phrase "the creative advance" (*PR* 32) is partly grounded on the asymmetry of the relation of prehension, where the property of asymmetry is expressible in terms of logical symbols.

These seven methods—use of generic philosophical concepts, comparison with other metaphysics, elaboration of internal coherence, application to empirical theories, examination of instances, imaginative generalization, and explication of formal structure—although not the only methods for understanding Whitehead's metaphysics, are important for my aim of understanding his ontology. Most important are elaboration of internal coherence (for disclosing the universal relation of synony) and explication of formal structure (for defining his types of entity). Emphasis on formal structure is not a diverting adjunct, because of a peculiarity in his metaphysics: although actual entities are the fundamental entities, we have no conscious acquaintance with any instance of them.

3. *A Problem: Finding an Instance of an Actual Entity*

My aim is to define Whitehead's types of entity by means of formal properties of the universal relation of synony (Chapter 3). While disclosing the universal relation of synony, I also interpret his types of entity informally (Chapter 2). For informal interpretations are necessary if formal definitions are to be adequate. In particular, when a type is defined, instances should be examined, for the definition must be adequate to the instances.

But the fundamental entities of Whitehead's ontology—the actual entities—are purely hypothetical, postulated by his metaphysics, but not known in any other way. We cannot observe an actual entity with our senses; we cannot infer an actual entity with empirical theories; we cannot consciously apprehend an actual entity through introspection. We must therefore obtain an understanding of actual entities through speculation, by using metaphors derived from the *societies* of actual entities that we can observe, infer, or introspect.

The enterprise of metaphysics is often charged with being transempirical; but usually the principles are conjectured, and applied to understand more fully the fundamental entities, some of which are already discerned. A peculiarity in Whitehead's metaphysics is that both the principles and the fundamental entities are known only through metaphysical speculation. For example, some of Aristotle's primary substances are observable—the man Socrates, the horse Bucephalus—even though others (perhaps) are not—individual bits of "pure" earth, air, fire, or water (the pure primary bodies). Also, Plato's "forms", although highly "speculative" to the unsympathetic reader of his dialogues, can allegedly be apprehended at the end of an arduous training in dialectical reasoning. Even Leibniz's esoteric doctrine of monads admits the direct acquaintance with one monad—one's own soul.

Although there is virtually no awareness among interpreters of

Whitehead's metaphysics that actual entities are known only through metaphysical speculation,[4] it is generally understood that ordinary human perception does not convey knowledge of an individual actual entity. Whitehead's theory of human perception is inordinately complex (see my Section 10); nevertheless, as a first approximation, it may be taken to imply that those entities which are perceived by the senses are always societies of actual entities, and never an individual actual entity, simply because some societies are large enough to be perceived, whereas their component actual entities are too small. For example, a stone, which is seen lying on the ground, is composed of actual entities which cannot be seen.

It may seem strange to assert that a stone is composed of actual entities, when, according to well-known empirical theories, a stone is composed of molecules, molecules are composed of atoms, and atoms are composed of elementary particles. But Whitehead does not intend to *replace* the hierarchy of composition that the natural sciences define; instead he speculates that the *ultimate* components in this hierarchy are actual entities (PR 136–167). Thus the elementary particles that are the components of the stone are themselves composed of actual entities (*PR* 150). In contrast, a physicist may project as a goal the discovery of the ultimate constituents of matter, but can only claim knowledge of those entities whose existence is empirically verified. Since Whitehead, in speculating that actual entities exist as the fundamental constituents of nature, leaps beyond the present limits of scientific knowledge, scientific theories cannot be used to infer the existence of his actual entities. Thus an instance of an actual entity cannot even be known indirectly by means of an empirical theory.

Although the verification of empirical theories is based on ordinary human perception, ordinary human perception is not the most primitive mode of conscious human experience. Rather, ordinary human perception—seeing, hearing, touching, etc.—is rooted in conscious, but vague, experiences of objects functioning causally, both the objects perceived, as they bring about our perception of them, and our bodily organs of perception, as they respond to the objects perceived (*PR* 179–184). But this "perception in the mode of causal efficacy" is extremely vague: no single actual entity is ever discriminated by it. (Whitehead explains this vagueness through his theory of "transmutation" [*PR* 40, 101].) For example, there is conscious awareness of the functioning of the eye in visual perception, but no conscious awareness of the functioning of one of the eye's component actual entities.

Causal perceptions of objects external to the perceiving human mind may indeed be vague, but surely the human mind, a linear series of actual entities (*PR* 163–167), can be conscious of a single "occasion" (i.e., finite actual entity) of its own self. Yet when we remember our own past experiences, we are not conscious of individual "actual occasions" of experience, but of experiences requiring a series of actual occasions for completion; the process of transmutation obscures not only our view of the world but our view of our own past as well. For example, memories of yesterday's experiences are obviously blurred, but even our consciousness of our own immediate past is of occasions, individually very fleeting, that are fused into useful social groupings, worthy of the attention of consciousness.

If the human mind cannot distinguish individual occasions of its past experiences, perhaps it can reflectively apprehend an actual occasion of its own present functioning. Yet Whitehead's theory of prehension requires the prehended entity to be in the past, for an (finite) actual entity cannot prehend itself (*PR* 130). Hence human self-consciousness is not a primitive but a highly derivative phenomenon: the present human mind, of which we are conscious through reflection, is an enduring object, an abstraction from its component actual entities, none of which prehends itself. Human self-consciousness, a paradigm for many metaphysics (*PR* 116), does not provide acquaintance with an instance of an actual entity.

Even if there is no instance of a finite actual entity that can be inspected independently of Whitehead's metaphysics, still there is an instance of an actual entity explicitly discussed in *Process and Reality:* God. Because religious experience is an alleged source of independent acquaintance with a deity, the method of examining instances might be applied. Nevertheless, since God is not a typical instance of an actual entity, it would be highly misleading to attempt to understand actual entities using just this one example (*PR* 521).[5] A proper use of the method of examining instances thus requires that instances of finite actual entities be made available for independent scrutiny, but, as we have seen, this cannot be done.

Since the human mind is not conscious of an instance of an (finite) actual entity, is there any relation between individual actual entity and human mind at all? The failure to discover an independent source of acquaintance with an instance of an actual entity compels us to seek an answer in Whitehead's metaphysics itself (*PR* 361–365): An actual entity must prehend each actual entity in its past. A prehension whose datum is a single actual entity rather than a nexus of actual entities is termed a "simple physical feeling". A complex physical feeling involving consciousness, whose datum is (part of) a society, is derived through a process of concrescence from simple physical feelings of the actual entities which are the components of the (part of the) society. Whereas the simple physical feelings are "devoid of consciousness" (*PR* 361), the conscious complex physical feeling, because of transmutation, feels the (part of the) society as one, without discriminating the component actual entities (*PR* 362, 387). Thus simple physical feelings, the links between individual actual entities and the human mind, always occur below the level of consciousness.[6]

Because an actual entity cannot be perceived, inferred empirically, experienced causally, remembered, or reflected upon, but can only be prehended below the level of consciousness, its graphic character, unfolded so explicitly, even if obscurely, on the pages of *Process and Reality,* is conveyed largely through metaphors. Since *societies* of actual entities *can* be perceived, inferred empirically, experienced causally, remembered, and reflected upon, concepts applying originally to such societies, and therefore acquired independently of Whitehead's metaphysics, can be imaginatively generalized to apply to actual entities. But implicit in these metaphysical metaphors are analogies between the societies from which the metaphors are derived and the actual entities to which the metaphors are applied. Because the societies can sometimes be examined, but not the actual entities, these analogies are one-sided. How, when groping with metaphors, can actual entities be defined?

4. *Understanding Whitehead's Ontology by Explicating Formal Structure*

Although actual entities are the "final realities" of which the world is composed, we are unable to examine any instances of them. Hence characterizing them in a metaphysics involves groping with metaphors whose appropriateness is problematical. But the metaphysics applies not only to actual entities but to all other entities as well. This complete generality of reference signals an implicit formal structure.

Disclosing the formal structure of the universe is a principal task of metaphysics. This formal structure can be expressed independently of the intrinsic properties of entities in the universe; the formal structure of the relations between entities can be expressed independently of the intrinsic nature of those relations. Therefore, even though the discovery of the intrinsic properties and relations of entities may require the examination of instances, formal structure may be disclosed without examining any instances at all (of entities of a given type).

But Whitehead's metaphysics is concerned with more than formal structure. His metaphysical categories formulate intrinsic properties and relations that are very general and therefore metaphysical. For example, although the relation of prehension exhibits a formal structure (e.g., asymmetry), it also has a descriptive content that is analogous to the intrinsic features of human experience. Thus the thesis that there is a formal structure implicit in Whitehead's metaphysics does not amount to the thesis that his metaphysics is nothing but (disguised) formal structure.

The formal structure of the universe consists in those "properties" (i.e., formal properties) of the universe expressible solely by logical signs. Since Whitehead's metaphysics is not purely formal, its adequate expression also requires signs that are descriptive (i.e., nonlogical). (The logical signs express formal properties of the metaphysical properties and relations expressed by the descriptive signs.) Thus metaphysical truths are expressed by a combination of logical and descriptive signs. For example, the sentence "If A prehends B, then B does not prehend A" contains the descriptive signs "A" and "B" which designate finite actual entities A and B, the descriptive sign "prehends" which designates the relation of prehension, and the logical signs "If . . . then . . ." and "not". (Thus the metaphysical relation of prehension possesses the formal property of asymmetry.)

Although a formal property of a metaphysical property or relation is expressible using logical signs, the fact that the metaphysical property or relation possesses that formal property is itself nonlogical ("empirical"). Metaphysical truths are not logical truths. The nature of asymmetry is independent of the nature of the universe, but the fact that prehension is asymmetric is confirmable or disconfirmable because of the nature of the universe. Thus logic may be used in metaphysics without turning metaphysics into a branch of logic.

Whitehead's metaphysics is both rich in metaphors and complex in structure. Rather than an exhaustive explication of the formal properties implicit in his metaphysics, I attempt only a partial explication. But a partial explication does not mean an explication of a part: it is not desirable, for example, to isolate the relation of prehension in order to analyze its formal structure, as if its coherence with other categories is not essential to its meaning. In particular, construing prehension merely as a relation whereby a prehending actual entity "reaches out" and "grasps" other actual entities neglects the internal process of concrescence whereby the prehending actual entity emerges as the unity of its prehensions.

Instead of a fragment, the proper subject of a partial explication is a metaphysical concept (or concepts) which underlies all the (relevant) categories. But the meaning of an underlying metaphysical concept does not exhaust the meaning of the categories which it underlies. Hence the formal properties implicit in an underlying metaphysical concept ground, but do not logically imply, the totality of formal properties implicit in the metaphysics.

Although Whitehead's criterion of coherence suggests that no metaphysical concept underlies any other, his "Category of the Ultimate" —that each actual entity is a novel entity created from the many entities which it unifies—is depicted as a category "presupposed" in all the other categories (*PR* 31–32). But the term "presupposed" is not elucidated; there is only the intimation that that which is presupposed is the more "general" and that which presupposes the more "special" (*PR* 31). From this we may surmise that, whenever one metaphysical concept underlies others, it is the more general and they the more specific.

There is such a profusion of categories in Whitehead's metaphysics that an underlying metaphysical concept need not be concentrated in a single category but may instead be dispersed into many. For example, prehension (*PR* 35) is a relation between an actual entity (the subject of the prehension) and other entities (the data of the prehension); ingression (*PR* 34) is a relation between an actual entity (that which is characterized) and an eternal object (that which characterizes); perhaps these common features of prehension and ingression mark an underlying metaphysical concept that is not expressed in a single category.

Since an unexpressed metaphysical concept underlying several categories may still be a fragment whose isolation would result in incoherence, the proper subject of a partial explication is a metaphysical concept (or concepts) which is so general as to underlie all the (relevant) categories. Specific metaphysical concepts applicable to specific categories may then be derived from the fully general metaphysical concept (or concepts) by chains of definitions. Thus an indistinct linear ordering of metaphysical concepts, proceeding from the general to the specific, is embedded in the more conspicuous circular ordering of the categories provided by coherence (and the even more conspicuous spiral ordering provided by discussions and applications [*PR* vii]).

I consider just one underlying metaphysical concept—the concept of synonty—which I express by a single descriptive sign. The explication of the formal structure implicit in this concept consists primarily in framing chains of definitions in terms of its formal properties. (Thus each sentence expressing a definition may be translated into a string of logical signs together with just the one descriptive sign.) My use of logic results in a definition "system" rather than an axiom system.

How is this underlying metaphysical concept of synonty to be disclosed? Substance—which is fundamental, for instance, in Aristotle's metaphysics—has inspired the use of the logic of (monadic) properties; conversely, Whitehead's view that process is fundamental and substance derivative, and his emphasis on the relational nature of reality, motivate the use of the logic of (dyadic) relations. Hence a clue for disclosing the concept of synonty is furnished by that category of Whitehead's metaphysics where "relations" are most manifest: the category of universal relativity (i.e., the "principle of relativity", category of explanation (iv)) (*PR* 33) (see my Section 5). The underlying metaphysical concept is thus the concept of a universal relation.

Since an underlying metaphysical concept must be so general as to underlie all the (relevant) categories, is it so general as to be vacuous? When we ascribe a (monadic) property to each and every entity, we risk saying nothing, because we assert no contrast. For example, if we hold that every entity is mental, then we establish no contrast with the nonmental (the physical), and therefore risk depriving the term "mental" of all its meaning. Yet when we ascribe a (dyadic) relation to each and every entity, we may thereby assert a significant contrast. For example, each entity can be prehended by some actual entity or other, but, in contrast, each actual entity cannot prehend each and every entity. The relation of prehension is thus ascribed to each and every entity in one sense, but, in contrast, not in another. Similarly, the universal relation of synonty holds of each and every entity without being vacuous: its formal properties serve to distinguish it from alternative relations that also hold of each and every entity. Hence an explication of the formal structure in Whitehead's metaphysics is strengthened by using the logic of relations rather than relying solely on the logic of (monadic) properties.

But the logic of relations is customarily expounded so as to be most pertinent to mathematics.[7] For example, the relation of identity among individuals (i.e., $x = y$), which is used to define cardinal numbers, is categorized in the logic of relations as an equivalence relation, that is, as a relation that is reflexive, symmetric, and transitive. In contrast, the logic of relations, as customarily expounded, is not so pertinent to some philosophical topics. For example, the relation of similarity among individuals, which might be used in epistemology to define perceived qualities, may be mistakenly categorized as an equivalence relation, because, even though it is symmetric and (perhaps) reflexive, it may be mistakenly categorized as transitive, when it is not (since there are cases such as the following: A feels as heavy as B, B feels as heavy as C, but A feels heavier than C). Thus the customary logic of relations must be developed to account for similarity relations—relations analogous to but weaker than equivalence relations—in order to be more pertinent to philosophy.[8] Therefore, the customary logic of relations must be developed in order to be more pertinent to Whitehead's metaphysics. For example, the relation of precedence (e.g., less than), which holds among members of a linear series of entities, and which is used in mathematics to define ordinal numbers, is irreflexive, asymmetric, transitive, and connected. In contrast, the relation of prehension, which, when restricted to finite actual entities, orders them (in that A precedes B in time if B prehends A), is irreflexive, asymmetric, transitive, but *not* connected, because some actual entities are contemporaneous (i.e., A is contemporaneous with B if A does not prehend B and B does not prehend A). In short, just as similarity is a relation analogous to but weaker than identity, prehension is a relation (among finite actual entities) analogous to but weaker than precedence.[9] The customary logic of relations, because designed for mathematics, is not especially germane to metaphysics, without further development. How, then, is logic—in particular, the logic of relations—to be used to explicate Whitehead's metaphysics?

The uses of logic in metaphysics have been quite divergent; compare, for example, Quine's "On What There Is"[10] with Kant's metaphysical deduction of the categories.[11] Perhaps the most striking use of logic has involved the use of logical inference to establish existence (e.g., the existence of a material world or a God). In particular, one realm of entities (e.g., sense-data) may ground an inference to the existence of another realm of entities (e.g., material things). Although such inferences have been discredited by theories of deduction associated with modern logic (because the conclusion does not yield anything that was not already in the premises), theories of definition associated with modern symbolic logic have prompted the superseding of inference by logical construction: instead of using one realm of entities to infer the ("real") existence of another, one realm is used to logically construct another (and thus to give it "fictional" existence). Moreover, an inveterate basis for both inference and construction has been the realm of entities that are immediately experienced or experiencible (e.g., impressions, sense-data, elementary experiences). Hence the inferential and constructional methods accord with the doctrine of the primacy of epistemology.

Since Whitehead seems to logically construct the entities of geometry (e.g., points and lines) on the basis of regions of space-time (*PR* 449–467), we might conjecture that the method of logical construction is appropriate for his metaphysical system generally.[12] For example, we might attempt to logically construct eternal objects on the basis of actual entities and their prehensions. Furthermore, the concept of experience is central to his metaphysics; hence the realm of immediately experiencible entities might be the primordial basis for logical construction. But the experiencible entities that are primordial are the entities experiencible (i.e., capable of being prehended) by all actual entities, not merely the entities consciously experiencible by those actual entities which comprise human minds; thus the entities that are experiencible are each and every entity in the universe (the category of universal relativity). But if all entities are experiencible, there is no realm of entities outside the realm of experiencible entities, and therefore there is no realm of entities that needs to be logically constructed on the basis of the experiencible entities. For example, eternal objects, actual entities, and prehensions are coequally experiencible; hence there is no need to logically construct eternal objects on the basis of the entities that are experiencible. The method of logical construction, in its customary form, is alien to Whitehead's metaphysics.

Instead of constructing some entities on the basis of others by means of logical processes of definition, Whitehead argues that some entities are constructed on the basis of others by means of real processes of nature. For example, an actual entity emerges as the final phase in the process of concrescence of its prehensions, and a complex prehension in an incomplete phase of that concrescence originates through the integration of prehensions in earlier phases. But why must we respect Whitehead's preference for real processes over logical constructions? In disregard of his intentions, we might therefore explicate his metaphysics by reinterpreting (or "reconstructing") real processes as logical constructions. For example, an actual entity might be reinterpreted as the class of its prehensions (in particular, as an equivalence class defined by some equivalence relation with prehensions as relata).[13] Nevertheless, my aim is not revision but disclosure; hence I examine only the formal structure that his metaphysics already contains, no matter how meager, rather than impose a structure on it that would alter its nature.

How may logic be used to explicate Whitehead's metaphysics without distorting it? An accurate explication must preserve the real processes whereby some entities come into being on the basis of others. But how can the immobility of logic be in harmony with the fluidity of process? The fluidity of process is reflected in a certain amorphousness in its metaphysical description. For example, we have noted that a process of concrescence yields complex prehensions in incomplete phases and an actual entity in the final phase; consequently, the process that produces an actual entity appears to have the same metaphysical character as the process that produces a complex prehension. How, then, are actual entities and prehensions to be distinguished? In sketching something like this problem (*PR* 28–29), Whitehead states that an actual entity has a kind of completeness that a prehension lacks; in particular, a prehension is incomplete because it refers beyond itself to the whole actual entity which is its subject. But a kind of incompleteness infests an actual entity as well; an actual entity refers beyond itself (through its "superjective" nature) to those actual entities in its future which prehend it (*PR* 41, 338–340). By further elaborating relations of coherence among the categories, the distinction between actual entities and prehensions could presumably be explained. But is this distinction so amorphous as to require such complex elaborations? Instead, I maintain that the distinction provided by coherence is grounded on a distinction provided by implicit formal structure. More precisely, I maintain that actual entities can be distinguished from prehensions by means of formal properties of the universal relation of synonty.

Thus logic is applicable to process because the entities created through real processes are divisible into ontological types by means of formal (logical) properties of the universal relation of synony. In contrast to the constructional method, where definitions are used to construct new types of entity, my "divisional" method employs definitions to distinguish into types the entities that are already presupposed. For example, let us consider the distinction between actual entities and eternal objects. In terms of coherence, actual entities are created, whereas eternal objects are eternal; eternal objects are the forms of definiteness ("universals") exemplified by actual entities; etc. How might logic ground this distinction? If the constructional method were used, actual entities might be presupposed, and eternal objects constructed, resulting in a variant of the familiar project of "reducing" universals to particulars.[14] In contrast, use of my "divisional" method involves presupposing both actual entities and eternal objects; accordingly, actual entities are distinguishable from eternal objects because (roughly) the creative advance of actual entities displays the formal property of asymmetry whereas the eternality of eternal objects displays the formal property of symmetry.

Whitehead's metaphysics applies to each and every entity in the universe; hence my aim is to divide all the entities in the universe into general ontological types by means of formal properties of the universal relation of synonty implicit in his metaphysics. Whitehead registers a list of basic types in his "Categories of Existence": actual entities, prehensions, nexūs, subjective forms, eternal objects, propositions, multiplicities, and contrasts. These types of entity are basic in that each entity in the universe is an instance of one and only one of them (*PR* 31). Thus societies do not comprise a basic type, because a society is a particular kind of nexus (*PR* 136–137). Whitehead then distinguishes each category of existence from the other categories of existence by means of relations of coherence with the whole system of categories (*PR* passim). As a consequence the list of categories of existence is corrected: a proposition, because it is the most important kind of contrast, is not really basic (*PR* 36), and a multiplicity of entities, because "it" is not a "proper" entity (i.e., a single entity) but rather many entities, is not really basic (*PR* 44–45). Consequently, the corrected list of basic types of entity (i.e., the corrected "Categories of Existence") is as follows: actual entities, prehensions, nexūs, subjective forms, eternal objects, and contrasts. Each ("proper") entity in the universe is an instance of one and only one of these basic types.

Since definitions are most clearly presented as dichotomies, it is convenient to define more inclusive types than the basic types. Because actual entities are the "final realities", all other entities—prehensions, nexūs, subjective forms, eternal objects, and contrasts—being derived from them, there is a dichotomy of actual entities and derivative entities. Only eternal objects (and God) are eternal; all other entities are created. Only God is infinite; all other entities are finite. Prehensions and subjective forms (also eternal objects and God), because ingredients of the internal process of concrescence of an actual entity, are "mental"; finite actual entities and nexūs (also contrasts), because external to the internal process of concrescence of an actual entity, are "physical". Hence the primary dichotomies are the infinite and the finite, the eternal and the created, the physical and the mental, and the actual and the derivative (Chapter 3). In short, my explication of the formal structure implicit in Whitehead's metaphysics orders the entities of the universe in a hierarchy of types from the general to the specific by means of a series of dichotomies that encompasses the basic "Categories of Existence".

Entities are divisible into primary dichotomies and basic types by means of formal properties of the universal relation of synonty implicit in Whitehead's metaphysics. How, then, is this universal relation of synonty to be made explicit? The abundance of basic types—actual entities, prehensions, nexūs, subjective forms, eternal objects, and contrasts—is matched by an abundance of special relations between entities of those types—for example, prehension, ingression, concrescence, and perception in the mode of presentational immediacy—all of which are more evident in Whitehead's metaphysics than the universal relation of synonty. The universal relation of synonty (which relates entities of all basic types to entities of all basic types) underlies some of these special relations—most importantly, prehension (which relates entities of all basic types to actual entities), ingression (which relates eternal objects to actual entities), patterning or diversity (which relates eternal objects to eternal objects), concrescence (which relates prehensions to prehensions, etc.), mutual sensitivity (which relates subjective forms to subjective forms, etc.), and synthesis (which relates entities of all basic types to contrasts). Therefore, through an investigation of a variety of more evident special relations, the universal relation of synonty is disclosed (Chapter 2).

The universal relation of synonty has a very general meaning that the special relations which it underlies have in common. "Synonty" means (roughly) a relation ("-y") of togetherness ("syn-") between

entities ("-ont-") (cf. "synchrony"). Hence each special relation
which synonty underlies can bring entities "together" (cf. the "Category of the Ultimate"). In particular, when one entity can have a
special relation which synonty underlies to another entity, the one
entity "has being for" the other entity. For example, when one actual entity can be prehended by another actual entity, the one actual entity has already come into being. Thus, in Whitehead's ontology, the "being" of entities is a relation between them. However,
when one entity can have a special relation which synonty underlies
to another entity, the one entity may not have the special relation
to the other entity. For example, although each eternal object can
ingress into any actual entity, a given eternal object may not ingress
into a given actual entity. Thus, when entities are synontic, they
have between them a special relation which synonty underlies only
"potentially" (cf. categories of explanation (vi) and (vii) [*PR* 34]).
Finally, when entities are synontic, they are together "directly"
("immediately").

When we investigate a special relation which synonty underlies,
we disclose synonty only in so far as it interrelates entities of the
basic types which can be interrelated by the special relation. Consequently, in order to disclose synonty adequately, we must examine
special relations which together can interrelate entities of all basic
types. More precisely, we must examine special relations which together can interrelate just those entities interrelated by synonty. For
the extension of synonty is identical with the union of the maximum possible ("potential") extensions of the special relations which
synonty underlies: On the one hand, if one entity can have a special
relation which synonty underlies to another entity, then the one entity is synontic to the other entity. For an implication of "underlying" is "inclusion of maximum possible extension". On the other
hand, if one entity is synontic to another entity, then the one entity
can have a special relation which synonty underlies to the other
entity. For a requisite of "disclosing" is "exhaustion of extension".
In short, one entity is synontic to another entity if and only if the
one entity can have a special relation which synonty underlies to
the other entity.

In summary, my aim is to divide the entities of Whitehead's ontology into primary dichotomies and basic types by means of formal
properties of a universal relation of synonty which underlies special
relations more evident in his metaphysics.

2

Relations Between Entities

5. A Clue: The Category of Universal Relativity

The category of universal relativity (i.e., the "principle of relativity", category of explanation (iv)), because it expresses the universal relatedness of entities, prefigures the universal relation of synonty.

The category of universal relativity may be understood most generally through generic philosophical concepts. Each entity in the universe is related to, but distinct from, every other entity. The universe is both an organic unity and a multiplicity of entities. Paradoxically, this universal relatedness of entities, expressed in the category of universal relativity, is the basis for their mutual distinctness (*PR* 224).

Actual entities are the foci of universal relatedness. Each actual entity is capable of prehending any entity that has already come into being; any eternal object can ingress into any actual entity. However, during its process of concrescence, an actual entity positively prehends only some of the already created entities, while eliminating others from positive relevance; and only some eternal objects ingress into it, others being incompatible for ingression. Even though each entity in the universe is related to every other, there are gradations of relevance (*PR* 224). That actual entities are foci of universal relatedness is the essence of the category of universal relativity.

That the category of universal relativity is central to Whitehead's metaphysics is suggested by surveying those pages of *Process and Reality* where that category is explicitly mentioned in respect of its relevance to traditional philosophical problems. According to Whitehead, the category may be used to clarify the distinction between universals and particulars (*PR* 76), to criticize the traditional doctrine of substance (*PR* 79–80), to justify his organic pluralism (*PR* 224), and to criticize the "sensationalist doctrine" (e.g., Hume's phenomenalism) (*PR* 252).

But the use of generic philosophical concepts and comparisons with other metaphysics only adumbrate the category of universal relativity. How are we to obtain a fuller understanding?

We are acquainted with no instance of an (finite) actual entity; hence the network of relationships that binds an actual entity to all other entities occurs below the level of consciousness and beyond the range of empirical theories. Nonetheless, we are acquainted with societies, some of which are bound together in networks of relationships that resemble the universal relatedness of actual entities. Therefore, concepts applying to the interrelatedness of societies, when imaginatively generalized, illuminate the category of the universal relativity of actual entities.

For example, let us consider the imaginative generalization of concepts applying to the interrelatedness of human beings. An actual entity is like a human being (both have "experiences", "mentality", etc.); a society of actual entities is like a society of human beings (both involve the transmission of a "defining characteristic" from member to member); the nexus of all actual entities is like the community of all mankind (both are bound together, at the very least, by certain "categorial" demands, which are, respectively, metaphysical and ethical). In a social group, each human being makes a difference to (has some degree of importance for, has an effect on) every other. Just as a moralist might extend this solidarity to all mankind (e.g., as universal brotherly love), Whitehead speculates that there is a togetherness of all actual entities through their prehensions of one another. But an actual entity as a focus of universal relatedness is also like a human being as a center of a sensory field; however, if we interpret each human being as having his own private sensory field, then the contents of each field are related "externally" by correlations to the contents of other fields; in contrast, an actual entity directly prehends the "contents" (i.e., prehensions) in other actual entities, and therefore is related to them "internally". Therefore, although there is an analogy between prehensions and our sensory experiences, it is more illuminating to understand prehensions by analogy with our experiences of other persons (*PR* 246). In Whitehead's metaphysics, sense perception is neither the ultimate basis for knowledge nor the best model for speculating about that basis.

The interrelatedness of human beings must be juxtaposed with additional sources of metaphor in order to sharpen our imaginative perception of the category of universal relativity. In particular, an

actual entity as a focus of universal relatedness is like a living or-
ganism as an outgrowth of its environment; just as organisms die
and are eaten, actual entities "perish" and are prehended. Hence a
prehended actual entity is not merely "represented" by but is "present in" ("immanent in") the prehending actual entity (*PR* 79–80).
In accordance with the category of universal relativity, an actual
entity engulfs its universe (*PR* 42).

Although the most noticeable sources of metaphor for Whitehead's metaphysical work in *Process and Reality* are human beings
and living organisms (e.g., the term "feeling" is a technical equivalent of "positive prehension" [*PR* 35], and a chapter is entitled "Organisms and Environment" [*PR* 168ff]), his earlier academic work
in physics and mathematics implanted the sources that are the most
deep-rooted. For example, just as a material particle is affected by
the gravitational field of every other particle in the universe (although for the most part negligibly), an actual entity prehends (and
therefore is affected by) every actual entity that has already come
into being (although for the most part negligibly) (*PR* 112). Why
are such metaphors from physics more deep-rooted than the metaphors from living organisms and human beings? Since a metaphysical explanation of the interrelatedness of human beings does not require the speculation that the actual entities comprising a human
mind prehend remote regions of empty space, the interrelatedness
of human beings merely resembles the universal relativity of actual
entities. In contrast, Whitehead's metaphysical grounding of gravita-
tion—that the transmission of gravitational forces is grounded on
the "transmission" of prehensions (and the inheritance of eternal objects) from actual entity to actual entity—requires that an actual
entity prehend the most remote of actual entities. Hence the all-
pervasiveness of gravitational fields not only resembles but is explained by (and therefore is evidence for) the universal relativity of
actual entities.

More deep-rooted than the metaphors from physics are the metaphors from mathematics, especially geometry. An actual entity must
prehend every actual entity that has already come into being, no
matter how near or remote; by analogy, any two points in a space,
no matter how close together or far apart, determine a unique line.
While the analogy with human beings suggests that an actual entity
should prehend only those actual entities in its neighborhood, the
deeper analogy with points suggests that the magnitude of separa-
tion makes no difference to the capacity to prehend (although it

may well make a difference to the degree of relevance). (The centrality of metaphors from geometry is evidenced in an early paper ["On Mathematical Concepts of the Material World" (1905)], where [in Concept V] Whitehead's projected definitions of material particles ["corpuscles"] in terms of linear elements ["linear objective reals"] prefigures his metaphysical doctrine that actual entities emerge through the concrescence of relations of prehension.[1]) But the system of lines in space not only resembles but is explained by the network of prehensions presupposed by the category of universal relativity. Among the many types of prehension, "strains" are prehensions that importantly involve geometrical forms (points, lines, etc.) in their objective data (*PR* 472). The system of lines in space (and therefore the "rest" and "motion" of the theory of relativity [*PR* 485ff]) is founded on the network of strains connecting all actual entities together. Even his theory of sense perception, in what might be a dangerous confusion of metaphor and application, is founded on strains (i.e., strains complex enough to "project" sensa) (see my Section 10). Geometry, more than any other special area of thought, is the most entangled in the structure of Whitehead's metaphysics.

In summary, Whitehead's category of the universal relativity of actual entities may be interpreted using metaphors derived from the interrelatedness of human beings, living organisms, material particles, points, or other suitable entities with which we are acquainted. Yet this imaginative illumination of universal relativity gives rise to a perplexity: although we are not acquainted with any instance of an actual entity, we are nonetheless acted upon by every actual entity that has ever come into being (*PR* 366). How is this perplexity to be clarified?

Even though we cannot consciously experience an actual entity, we ("preconsciously") prehend every actual entity that has ever come into being. For example, we see a stone lying on the ground; the stone is composed of actual entities; but we do not see any actual entities; nonetheless, we (preconsciously) prehend the (past) actual entities of the stone (and every other actual entity that has already come into being). Analogously, the stone is composed of electrons (and other elementary particles); but we do not see any electrons; nonetheless, some of these electrons emit photons of light that cause us to see the stone. But the causal interaction of stone and mind (through electromagnetic particles or waves) not only resembles but is explained by the interrelatedness of actual entities of stone and mind (through prehensions). More generally, the all-pervasiveness of electromagnetic fields not only resembles but is explained by the universal relativity of actual entities (*PR* 53–54). Therefore, the category of universal relativity elucidates the causal origins of vision. But why must Whitehead hold a causal theory of perception? Whitehead speculates that there is no "bifurcation of nature" into objects of science (entities "in" nature) and human minds (entities "outside" nature); instead, electrons, stones, and human minds are coequally composed of actual entities. Since physics requires the universal interrelatedness of actual entities, and since we (i.e., our minds) are bound up in that interrelatedness, we must (preconsciously) prehend every actual entity that has ever come into being, even though we cannot see any. In summary, application to empirical theories of visual perception helps to clarify the significance of the category of universal relativity.

Interpreting the category of universal relativity through metaphors and applications risks surfeiting our understanding. We must now trace pathways of coherence through the map of categories in order to delineate the features of the universal relation of synonty.

Whitehead states the category of universal relativity as follows:

"(iv) That the potentiality for being an element in a real concrescence of many entities into one actuality, is the one general metaphysical character attaching to all entities, actual and non-actual; and that every item in its universe is involved in each concrescence. In other words, it belongs to the nature of a 'being' that it is a potential for every 'becoming.' This is the 'principle of relativity.' " (*PR* 33)

How is this statement of the category to be interpreted? There is a general metaphysical principle that attaches to entities. It is so general that it attaches to all entities, both actual and nonactual. What is this metaphysical principle? Each entity has the potentiality for being an element in a real concrescence of many entities into one actuality. The *one actuality* into which the many entities concresce is an actual entity. An entity is an *element* in a real concrescence into one actual entity if it is positively prehended by or if it ingresses into that actual entity. The *many entities* that concresce into one actual entity are, in one sense, all the elements in that concrescence, that is, all the entities that are positively prehended by or ingress into that actual entity. But, in another sense, the *many entities* that concresce into one actual entity are, not the entities prehended, but the prehensions of those entities. Thus the *real concrescence* of many entities into one actual entity is the internal process whereby those prehensions come together into a unity. Each entity has the *potentiality* for being prehended by or ingressing into an actual entity. But some entities need not be elements in the internal process of concrescence of an actual entity. In summary, each entity has the potentiality for being prehended by or ingressing into an actual entity; each entity has the potentiality for being an element in the internal process of concrescence of an actual entity; but some entities are excluded from that concrescence.

To which entities does this metaphysical character attach? Every item in an actual entity's universe is involved in each concrescence. But not all entities are items in every actual entity's universe. The universe of an actual entity, *its universe,* is its "actual world" (*PR* 33–34): the created entities that have already come into being and all the eternal objects. Therefore, it does not belong to the nature of a *created* "being" that it is a potential for *every* "becoming"; rather, it belongs to the nature of a created "being" that it is a potential for every *future* "becoming". In other words, when a created entity comes into being, it is a potential for every actual entity that has yet to come into being, but not for any actual entity that has already come into being. Therefore, this one general metaphysical character attaches to all entities, actual and nonactual, in the following sense: it belongs to the nature of *every* "being" that it is a potential for *some* "becoming". This is the category of universal relativity.

In contrast to my exposition of the quoted statement of the category of universal relativity, my interpretation of the category of universal relativity using metaphors derived from the interrelatedness of societies implies that each entity in the actual world of an actual entity not only has the *potentiality* for being prehended but *is* prehended by that actual entity. How is this discrepancy to be explained? If an entity has the potentiality for being prehended by an actual entity, it must either be *included* as an element in the concrescence of that actual entity by being prehended *positively* (i.e., "felt"), or, be *excluded* from that concrescence by being prehended *negatively;* it cannot be neglected. Therefore, whether prehended positively or negatively, the entity is always relevant to that actual entity. In short, the potentiality for prehension always results in a positive prehension (i.e., a "feeling") or a negative prehension (*PR* 66). Hence my interpretation by metaphors and my exposition of the quoted statement elicit different aspects of the same principle.

The category of universal relativity is more clearly understood by surveying its applicability to entities of the various ontological types. Each entity in the actual world of an actual entity has the potentiality for being prehended by or ingressing into that actual entity (the category of universal relativity). As a consequence, each *actual* entity in the actual world of an actual entity has the potentiality for being prehended by that latter actual entity (application of the category to actual entities). But not all actual entities are in the actual world of that actual entity (*PR* 33–34, 101). In general, for any two (finite) actual entities A and B, either A has the potentiality for being prehended by B and B does not have the potentiality for being prehended by A (thus A is in B's past), or A does not have the potentiality for being prehended by B and B has the potentiality for being prehended by A (thus A is in B's future), or A does not have the potentiality for being prehended by B and B does not have the potentiality for being prehended by A (thus A and B are contemporaneous). Accordingly, the realization of a prehension presupposes the potentiality for being prehended; in the absence of this potentiality, there can be no prehension at all. The concept of the potentiality for being prehended grounds the distinction between prehension and nonprehension.

The distinction between prehension and nonprehension is different from the distinction between positive prehension and negative prehension. If an entity has the potentiality for being prehended by an actual entity, then it is prehended (either positively or negatively) by that actual entity; but if it does not have the potentiality for being prehended by that actual entity, then it is not prehended by that actual entity at all. In contrast to the absence of prehension, a negative prehension is a definite bond.

Each *derivative created* entity (i.e., each prehension, nexus, subjective form, and contrast) in the actual world of an actual entity has the potentiality for being prehended by that actual entity (application of the category of universal relativity to derivative created entities). But not all derivative created entities are in the actual world of that actual entity. In general, for any created entity (i.e., derivative created entity or finite actual entity) A and finite actual entity B, either A is in B's past, or A is in B's future, or A and B are contemporaneous (or A concresces into B). Moreover, a derivative created entity is derived from actual entities; correspondingly, a positive prehension of a derivative created entity is derived from positive prehensions of actual entities. For example, a nexus is a multiplicity of actual entities that are interrelated by their prehensions of one another; correspondingly, a complex physical feeling of a nexus is produced through the integration of simple physical feelings of the actual entities in the nexus. Consequently, in order that a derivative created entity in the actual world of an actual entity have the potentiality for being prehended by that actual entity, the actual entities from which that derivative created entity is derived *must* be *positively* prehended (i.e., felt) by that actual entity (*PR* 335). In general, every actual entity in the actual world of an actual entity must be positively prehended by that actual entity. Actual entities are universally interconnected through their simple physical feelings of one another.

Each *eternal object* in the actual world of an actual entity has the potentiality for being *prehended* by that actual entity (application of the category of universal relativity to eternal objects). Whereas each created entity is created (i.e., comes into being), each eternal object is eternal (i.e., does not come into being but is always in being). Therefore, although not all created entities are in the actual world of that actual entity (because not all created entities have come into being when that actual entity comes into being), all eternal objects are in the actual world of that and every actual entity (because all eternal objects are always in being) (*PR* 34). However, since some eternal objects are more relevant than others to that actual entity, each eternal object is prehended either positively or negatively by that actual entity. Moreover, an eternal object is a derivative entity, because it cannot exist apart from actual entities, but must ingress into some actual entity somewhere; correspondingly, a conceptual prehension of an eternal object is abstracted from physical prehensions of actual entities into which that eternal object ingresses. In short, each eternal object has the potentiality for and realizes a determinate bond of positive or negative conceptual prehension with every actual entity.

Each eternal object is prehended by every actual entity. In contrast, each created entity is prehended only by those actual entities in its future. This contrast between the application of the category of universal relativity to eternal objects and its application to created entities is grounded on the distinction between always in being (eternality) and coming into being (becoming). The indeterminateness of the future is at the heart of Whitehead's metaphysics.

Each *eternal object* has the potentiality for *ingressing* into any actual entity (further application of the category of universal relativity to eternal objects). But not all eternal objects ingress into each actual entity. In particular, if a given eternal object ingresses into a given actual entity, then eternal objects incompatible with that eternal object are excluded from ingressing (in that respect) into that actual entity (*PR* 367). For example, eternal objects ingress when prehended positively, and are excluded from ingressing (as data of prehension) when prehended negatively. But eternal objects also ingress (or are excluded from ingressing) into actual entities as abstract characteristics (i.e., properties and relations) of those actual entities. Thus each eternal object has the potentiality for realizing several different modes of ingression into any actual entity (*PR* 249, 445).

The category of universal relativity, because it expresses the universal relatedness of entities, prefigures the universal relation of synonty. But the universal relatedness expressed in the category of universal relativity has actual entities as foci. By generalizing this universal relatedness, we obtain a principle that "it belongs to the nature of a 'being' that it is a potential for entities of all types (not just actual entities)". Thus a principle of universal relatedness through synonty is derived from the category of universal relativity by imaginative generalization.

When an entity can be prehended by an actual entity, the entity has already come into being (if created) (*PR* 356) or is always in being (if eternal). Analogously, when one entity is synontic to another entity, the one entity has being for the other entity. Thus the very general meaning that the universal relation of synonty has in common with the special relations which it underlies concerns the "being" of the entities related.

Although each eternal object has the potentiality for ingressing into any actual entity, a given eternal object may not ingress into a given actual entity. Analogously, when one entity is synontic to another entity, the one entity is merely a "potential" for the other entity. Thus entities which are synontic can have but may not have between them a special relation which synonty underlies.

Contemporaneous actual entities cannot prehend each other. Nonetheless, their actual worlds overlap: Given two contemporaneous actual entities A and B, there is a third actual entity C such that C can be prehended by A and C can be prehended by B (and there is a fourth actual entity D such that A can be prehended by D and B can be prehended by D). But this indirect linkage by relations of prehension is not itself a relation of prehension. Analogously, when one entity is synontic to another entity, they are together "immediately" ("directly"); there is no third entity which "mediates" between them in order to make them synontic. Thus, when one entity is related not directly but only indirectly to another entity by the special relations which synonty underlies, the one entity is not synontic to the other entity. In particular, contemporaneous actual entities are not synontic.

Prehension and ingression are special relations which the universal relation of synonty underlies. Therefore, if an entity can be prehended by an actual entity, then the entity is synontic to the actual entity, and, if an eternal object can ingress into an actual entity, then the eternal object is synontic to the actual entity. But synonty, a universal relation, relates entities of each type to entities of every type. How, then, are entities of each type related to entities other than actual entities? How, for example, are eternal objects related to one another?

6. *The Relational Essence of Eternal Objects*

Preoccupied with the role of eternal objects in the concrescence of actual entities, Whitehead neglects the relations of eternal objects to one another. Hence we must piece together an account from a few scattered comments.

An eternal object is a form of definiteness (*PR* 32). How is one form of definiteness related to another? There is an endless variety of forms. Are the relations of forms to one another therefore endlessly various? Is there a general relation underlying the variety of specific relations? Can the problem of finding a general relation be dealt with in abstraction from particular instances? Whitehead's theory of eternal objects is so shrouded in generality that the proper starting point must be an examination of instances.

A gauge of the obscurity of *Process and Reality* is the scarcity of recorded instances of eternal objects. Red and blue (*PR* 349), color (*PR* 296), straight line (*PR* 472), and the "any" of logic (*PR* 245) are among the few eternal objects mentioned. But a multitude of types of eternal object is recorded, for example, sounds (*PR* 96, 357), geometrical forms (*PR* 472), emotions (*PR* 446), belief-characters (*PR* 408), relations (*PR* 349–350), and general principles (*PR* 296). Hence additional instances may be tentatively inferred: middle *C*, square, anger, certitude, is next to, and the universal relation of synonty.

How are these instances of eternal objects related to one another? We may tentatively infer that red is related to blue by relative position on the color spectrum, that red is related to color by the relation of species to genus (subsumption), that red is related to straight line by the relation of color to shape, that red is related to "any" by the relation of value to universally quantified variable (instantiation), etc. Is there a general relation underlying such diverse relations as these?

As an underlying generality, Whitehead distinguishes eternal objects into two metaphysical types: the "objective" species and the "subjective" species (*PR* 445–447). Eternal objects that can ingress into the subjective form of a prehension—e.g., red, blue, color, middle *C,* anger, and certitude—are of the subjective species, whereas eternal objects that cannot ingress into the subjective form of a prehension but can only ingress into the objective datum—e.g., straight line, square, and is next to—are of the objective species. (It is not clear how the more abstract eternal objects—e.g., "any" and the universal relation of synonty—fit into this classification.) However, this general distinction among eternal objects is founded on a distinction between modes of ingression, and does not expose to view any general relation of eternal objects to one another.

Whitehead also distinguishes eternal objects into sensa and patterns (*PR* 174–176). Is this distinction also founded on modes of ingression? According to traditional epistemology, a sensum (or sense-datum) is that of which we are immediately aware in an act of sensation. Moreover, it is ambiguous as to whether a sensum is a particular (e.g., a color patch) or a universal (e.g., a color). Construing sensa as universals (i.e., eternal objects), instances of sensa are red (or particular shades of red) and middle *C.* Are these sensa of traditional epistemology the sensa of Whitehead's metaphysics?

Sensa occur in patterns. For instance, middle *C* may occur in the chord *CEG* (the *C* major triad). If just middle *C* is sounded on a piano, we hear middle *C* without hearing the chord *CEG;* but if the chord *CEG* is sounded, we must hear, if not middle *C,* at least some *C.* Whitehead's distinction between sensa and patterns is generalized from instances such as this distinction between the hearing of middle *C* and the hearing of *CEG:* a sensum can ingress separately from the ingression of any pattern, whereas a pattern must ingress together with sensa that it patterns (*PR* 175–176).

Although founded on modes of ingression, the distinction between sensa and patterns exposes to view relations of eternal objects to one another. Middle *C* (an eternal object) is a component of the chord *CEG* (an eternal object). In general, sensa are components of patterns. In Whitehead's language, a pattern is a "manner of relatedness" (*PR* 174), whereas sensa are the "matter" related (*PR* 175). Moreover, the chord *CEG* exemplifies the general pattern "given tone together with its third and fifth" (the "common chord"). Accordingly, just as sensa are components of patterns, patterns are components of patterns. Is this relation of patterning (i.e., *x* is a component of the pattern *y*) between sensa and pattern and between patterns and pattern a general relation that all eternal objects have with one another?

According to traditional epistemology, middle *C* is a sensum. However, according to Whitehead's metaphysics, middle *C* is *not* a sensum. When middle *C* is sounded on a piano, we hear a complex datum analyzable into several patterns of sensa, including a qualitative pattern of fundamental tone and overtones and a quantitative pattern of intensities (cf. the example of "the audition of sound" at *PR* 357–358). Therefore, although we are conscious of the patterns of sensa (i.e., the complex eternal object consisting of patterns together with sensa) in a complex datum such as middle *C*, we need not be conscious of sensa individually (e.g., we need not be conscious of an overtone [assuming an overtone is a sensum]). Whereas the traditional definitions of "sensum" are in terms of consciousness (or physiology), Whitehead's definition is in terms of metaphysical principles (*PR* 175). But if Whitehead's sensa are not the ordinary sensa, what are they?

Whitehead's concept of "sensa" may be understood as an imaginative generalization of the traditional concept of "sensa". Moreover, just as prehensions are like human experiences, although human experiences are not prehensions (because we are conscious of human beings and their experiences whereas we are not conscious of actual entities and their prehensions), Whitehead's sensa are like traditional sensa, although traditional sensa need not be instances of Whitehead's sensa. Similarly, Whitehead's concept of "patterns" may be understood as an imaginative generalization of the concept of patterns of traditional sensa. Therefore, his relation of patterning may itself be understood on analogy with relations of patterning exemplified in patterns of traditional sensa.

But Whitehead's sensa and patterns are understandable through other analogies, for example, the analogy with subjects and predicates. In particular, we may conjecture that Whitehead, an author of *Principia Mathematica,* intended an analogy between the hierarchy of patterns in his metaphysics and the hierarchy of functions in the theory of logical types. Why, then, did he choose to emphasize the analogy with the sensa and patterns of traditional epistemology? Eternal objects of the subjective species ingress into the subjective forms of an actual entity's prehensions. Since an actual entity's subjective forms express its "emotional reactions" (metaphor) to what it prehends, these eternal objects of the subjective species are (analogous to) emotions, intensities, adversions, aversions, pleasures, pains, etc. (*PR* 446). During the concrescence of an actual entity's prehensions, the subjective forms of those prehensions are integrated together, with the result that the eternal objects in those subjective forms are joined together into patterns (*PR* 359–360) (cf. Whitehead's use of the term "emotional pattern" at *PR* 417–420). In short, eternal objects of the subjective species are "emotional" sensa and "emotional" patterns (and thus are analogous to so-called "tertiary qualities"). Consequently, since his theory of eternal objects is designed to be especially appropriate to his theory of subjective forms, Whitehead's sensa and patterns are particularly elucidated by analogy with that of which we are immediately aware in acts of *inner* sensation.

Whitehead's sensa and patterns, while partially understood in terms of analogies with traditional sensa and patterns, are defined quite generally in terms of metaphysical principles. Does his relation of patterning therefore hold among eternal objects generally? In order to elucidate the generality of the relation of patterning, we must make explicit the generality of his metaphysical definitions of sensa and patterns. Sensa can ingress separately from patterns, whereas patterns must ingress together with sensa. But why can sensa ingress separately from patterns? A pattern is a manner of relatedness between eternal objects that it patterns; therefore, when it ingresses, eternal objects that it patterns must also ingress. In contrast, a sensum is not a manner of relatedness between eternal objects, but can only be a relatum in patterns; therefore, when it ingresses, no eternal objects ingress as its relata, and, even though it usually ingresses together with patterns in which it is a relatum, it need not ingress together with patterns in which it is a relatum (*PR* 176). Consequently, the distinction between sensa and patterns in terms of modes of ingression presupposes a distinction in terms of the relatedness of eternal objects with one another. In short, patterns are distinguished from sensa because patterns are manners of relatedness between eternal objects whereas sensa are not manners of relatedness between eternal objects (*PR* 174). The metaphysical definitions of sensa and patterns are founded on a general concept of relatedness between eternal objects.

There is a general relation of patterning that eternal objects have with one another: each eternal object has relations of patterning (i.e., *x* is a component of the pattern *y*) with other eternal objects. Moreover, each eternal object has potential relations of patterning that it need not realize in a given ingression. For example, when the chord *CEG* is sounded at the one-line octave on a piano, middle *C* realizes a relation of patterning with *CEG*, but, although it has the potentiality for a relation of patterning with the chord CE^bG (the *C* minor triad), it does not realize a relation of patterning with CE^bG. In general, each eternal object has potentialities of relationship with other eternal objects which Whitehead terms its "relational essence" (*PR* 175). Therefore, there is a relativity among eternal objects that is analogous to the universal relativity of actual entities: each eternal object has the potentiality for being a component of patterns. But does each eternal object have the potentiality for being a component of every pattern?

There are relations of diversity between eternal objects (*PR* 392). For example, when the chord *CEG* is sounded at the one-line octave on a piano, middle *C* realizes a relation of patterning with *CEG*, but the tone that is a whole step above middle *C*, call it "middle *D*", does not realize a relation of patterning with *CEG*. Furthermore, middle *D* can never be a component of *CEG*. In short, there is a relation of diversity between middle *D* and *CEG*. Also, when *CEG* is sounded on a piano, it does not have the color red as a component, and can never have the color red as a component; there is a relation of diversity between the color red and *CEG*. But can we not imagine a "possible world" in which the color red is realized as a component of *CEG*? *CEG* is itself a component of the general pattern "a given sensory quality together with a second sensory quality which is a short interval from the first together with a third sensory quality which is the same interval from the second". There are other potential components of this general pattern, some of which have not been realized in our universe; in particular, we may attempt to imagine the following pattern (or something like it): "a given tone or color together with a second tone or color which is a short interval from the first together with a third tone or color which is the same interval from the second" (call it a "chord-spectrum"). Therefore, when we think that we are imagining a "possible world" in which the color red occurs in a chord, we are really imagining that the color red occurs in something like a "chord-spectrum". In short, even though the multiplicity of eternal objects contains a variety of imaginable patterns not realized in our universe, there are relations of diversity between eternal objects.

In conclusion, the relational essence of an eternal object is its potentialities for patterning and diversity. Therefore, there is a universal relativity among eternal objects that is analogous to the universal relativity of actual entities: each eternal object has the potentiality for being in a relation of patterning with or diversity from each other eternal object. The general relation that all eternal objects have with one another is the relation "patterning or diversity".

As addenda to this elaboration of the theory of eternal objects, let us enquire into the role of God and the relevance of *Science and the Modern World*. Just as the potentiality for being prehended must be realized by a prehension (whether positive or negative), the potentiality for patterning or diversity must be realized. Since not all eternal objects are realized in (i.e., ingress into) the world of finite actual entities, the multiplicity of eternal objects, together with their relations of patterning and diversity, must be realized in God's "primordial nature" (i.e., must be conceptually prehended by God) (*PR* 73). Moreover, God, an actual entity in the actual world of each finite actual entity, is prehended by each finite actual entity, and thereby gives to each finite actual entity its "initial subjective aim", a selection of eternal objects that are most relevant to it (*PR* 46–50). Why did I make explicit the general interrelatedness of eternal objects without remarking on this metaphysical role of God? Each *finite* actual entity in the actual world of a finite actual entity, when prehended by that finite actual entity, *also* gives to that finite actual entity a selection of eternal objects that are relevant to its process of concrescence (*PR* 46). However, God gives the eternal objects that are most relevant. In other words, both God and finite actual entities exemplify the metaphysical principle that conceptual prehensions of eternal objects are derived from physical prehensions of actual entities (*PR* 337). Therefore, God is not invoked as a metaphysical *principle* to explain what other metaphysical principles fail to explain; rather, God is merely an *instance* of the metaphysical principles, albeit the "chief exemplification" (*PR* 134–135, 343–344, 521). Consequently, in elaborating the internal coherence of metaphysical principles generally—in particular, when making explicit the interrelatedness of eternal objects and their ingression into actual entities generally—it is not always necessary to remark on the role of God.

In his "Abstraction", the tenth chapter of *Science and the Modern World,* Whitehead outlined a theory of the structure of the relatedness of eternal objects with one another.[2] Why did I make explicit the general interrelatedness of eternal objects without making use of this chapter? "Abstraction" is very abstract. Unraveling the terse definitions in which the structure in "Abstraction" is expressed is itself a major project. Moreover, there are discrepancies between the metaphysics adumbrated in the earlier work *Science and the Modern World* (originally published in 1925) and the system of categories elaborated in the later work *Process and Reality* (1929), probably because the system of categories was still under construction when *Science and the Modern World* was written. Therefore, even if the structure in "Abstraction" were clarified, its relevance to the theory of eternal objects in *Process and Reality* would still be problematic. Nonetheless, we may conjecture that the structure in "Abstraction", because founded on the thesis that each eternal object has a relational essence, partially confirms my contention that eternal objects are interrelated by patterning or diversity.

The principle of the general interrelatedness of eternal objects is analogous to the category of universal relativity. Just as each entity in the actual world of an actual entity can be prehended by or ingress into that actual entity, so each eternal object can be in a relation of patterning with or diversity from every other eternal object. Hence the very general meaning of the universal relation of synonty is disclosed in the special relation of patterning or diversity: each eternal object, because eternal, has being for every other eternal object. Thus synonty underlies patterning or diversity as well as prehension and ingression. What, then, are additional relations which synonty underlies?

Derivative created entities are related to actual entities by the relation of prehension. But how are derivative created entities related to one another? In particular, how are prehensions, the most fundamental type of derivative created entity, related to one another?

7. *The Concrescence of Prehensions*

An actual entity is a "concrescence of prehensions" (category of explanation (x) [*PR* 35]). More precisely, an actual entity comes into being through an internal process involving the concrescence (i.e., the "growing together") of its prehensions (categories of explanation (i), (ii), (xxvii), (xxv) [*PR* 33, 39, 38]). Thus prehensions are related to one another through their concrescence into an actual entity.

Absorbed in comparisons with other metaphysics and applications to empirical theories in Part II of *Process and Reality* ("Discussions and Applications"), Whitehead does not clearly expound his theory of the concrescence of prehensions until Part III ("The Theory of Prehension") (but also see *PR* 127–136, 317–328). Because expounded in Part III by means of the internal coherence of the system of categories, his theory of concrescence is a perplexing mosaic of concepts. How, then, are we to understand the relations of prehensions to one another? [3]

We may understand the relations of prehensions to one another in an actual entity on analogy with the relations of actual entities to one another in the universe (*PR* 327, 347–348). Just as the universe is a "creative advance" involving a succession of actual entities (*PR* 31–32), so an actual entity is a "concrescence" involving a succession of phases of prehensions (*PR* 39). Accordingly, just as an actual entity comes into being from the actual entities in its actual world, so a prehension comes into being from prehensions in earlier phases. Thus there is a universal relatedness of prehensions in an actual entity that is analogous to the universal relatedness of actual entities in the universe.

Prehensions concresce through a succession of phases into an actual entity. Thus prehensions are related to one another by coming into being in phases. How, therefore, are we to understand the phases of concrescence? There are three main phases in the concrescence of an actual entity: the initial phase (of simple physical feelings), the supplementary phases (of conceptual prehensions and integral prehensions), and the final phase (the actual entity as a completed unity of feeling) (*PR* 323). Accordingly, in any supplementary phase or in the initial phase (i.e., in any incomplete phase) there are a multiplicity of prehensions (categoreal obligation (i) [*PR* 39]), whereas in the final phase there is a single (i.e., a "proper") entity (namely, the completed actual entity) (*PR* 38).

In the initial phase of an actual entity's concrescence, a multiplicity of simple physical feelings come into being (*PR* 362). A simple physical feeling comes into being through a process of "transition" (*PR* 319–320) involving the "absorption" of a past actual entity by means of one of that past actual entity's prehensions (*PR* 361). Thus an actual entity "conforms" to (is the "effect" of) the actual entities in its actual world through its initial phase of simple physical feelings (*PR* 361–365).

In the first supplementary phase of an actual entity's concrescence, a multiplicity of conceptual prehensions come into being (*PR* 378). A conceptual prehension comes into being in the first supplementary phase through a process of "derivation" from a simple physical feeling in the initial phase (*PR* 39–40, 378–382). In particular, the conceptual prehension of an eternal object is derived from a simple physical feeling of an actual entity into which the eternal object has ingression. However, in so deriving a conceptual prehension of an eternal object, an actual entity makes its own "valuation" of it (*PR* 367–369). Whereas in its initial phase an actual entity "conforms" to the actual entities in its actual world, in its first supplementary phase it begins its "aim" at its own "private ideal" (*PR* 323, 369).

In any succeeding supplementary phase of an actual entity's concrescence, a multiplicity of integral prehensions come into being (*PR* 365–366). An integral prehension comes into being in a supplementary phase through a process of "integration" of prehensions which have already come into being in earlier phases (*PR* 39, 322–323, 337). For example, a (pure) complex physical feeling of a nexus comes into being through the integration of simple physical feelings of the actual entities in the nexus (*PR* 350–353). The spectrum of types of integral prehension, from the most rudimentary to the most complex, includes physical purposes (*PR* 380, 406, 420–428), complex physical feelings (of nexūs), propositional feelings (see my Section 9), transmuted feelings (*PR* 40, 382–389), "prehensions" in the mode of presentational immediacy (see my Section 10), and intellectual feelings (*PR* 406–420). Integral prehensions promote an actual entity's aim at "intensity" of "satisfaction" (*PR* 41, 402, 416); thus the spectrum of types of integral prehension corresponds to a spectrum of types of satisfaction (*PR* 129–130, 169–170). In its supplementary phases of integral prehensions, an actual entity continues its aim at its "private ideal".

In the final phase (i.e., the "satisfaction") of an actual entity's concrescence, the actual entity itself comes into being as a complex unity of feeling (*PR* 38, 39, 129, 334–340). Therefore, the many prehensions of a given entity in the incomplete phases must be integrated together to produce a single prehension of that entity in the final phase (*PR* 39, 347). For example, suppose that actual entity *A* feels actual entities *B* and *C*, that *B* also feels *C*, and that, in feeling *B*, *A* feels *B*'s feeling of *C;* in a later phase of concrescence, *A* must, therefore, integrate its diverse feelings of *C* into a single feeling (*PR* 345–346). (Moreover, the many prehensions of a given eternal object must be integrated into a single conceptual prehension of that eternal object (*PR* 346–347, 367).) Accordingly, the actual entities in the actual world of an actual entity, because they prehend one another, comprise a nexus; an actual entity, in having simple physical feelings of the actual entities in its actual world, has many prehensions of the nexus of those actual entities; therefore, in its final phase of concrescence, an actual entity must be a complex unity of feeling of the nexus of actual entities in its actual world (together with all the other entities implicated in that nexus) (*PR* 351–352). In short, by means of the process of integration, prehensions concresce (i.e., grow together) into an actual entity (*PR* 347–348).

God, the "chief exemplification" of metaphysical principles, is an actual entity with phases of concrescence. Nonetheless, his phases are the "converse" of a finite actual entity's (*PR* 529, 134–135, 524). In a finite actual entity's initial phase there are physical feelings of actual entities, whereas in God's "initial phases" (i.e., in his "primordial nature") there are conceptual feelings of eternal objects (*PR* 46–50, 521–523). In a finite actual entity's supplementary phases there are conceptual feelings effecting integrations of physical feelings, whereas in God's "supplementary phases" (i.e., in his "consequent nature") there are physical feelings of finite actual entities (*PR* 46–47, 523–531). In a finite actual entity's final phase there is a completed unity of feeling (its "perishing"), whereas in God's ("everlasting") succession of "final phases" (i.e., in his "superjective nature") he is prehended by the succession of finite actual entities (*PR* 134–135, 343–344, 532). Therefore, my discussion of Whitehead's theory of concrescence applies strictly to finite actual entities and only approximately to God (*PR* 521).

How, then, are prehensions related to one another through their concrescence into an actual entity? The internal process of concrescence of an actual entity involves the process of derivation (of conceptual prehensions) and the process of integration (of integral prehensions and of the completed (finite) actual entity). Therefore, each prehension in an incomplete phase is involved in processes of concrescence (derivation or integration) which produce prehensions in later phases (and the completed actual entity in the final phase). More compactly, each prehension concresces into other prehensions (and into the completed actual entity). Consequently, from the concept of an internal process of concrescence, I abstract the concept of a "relation of concrescence" (i.e., x concresces into y).

The succession of phases of prehensions in the concrescence of an actual entity is such that each phase in the succession is either "earlier" or "later" than each other phase. Accordingly, when a prehension comes into being in an incomplete phase, every prehension in every earlier phase has already come into being, and no prehension in any later phase has yet come into being. Therefore, by analogy with the category of universal relativity, each prehension in an incomplete phase has the potentiality for concrescing into any prehension in any later phase (and into the completed actual entity). (But no prehension in an incomplete phase has the potentiality for concrescing into any prehension in any earlier phase.) Thus there is a universal relatedness of prehensions in an actual entity that is analogous to the universal relatedness of actual entities in the universe. Consequently, the very general meaning of the universal relation of synonty is disclosed in the special relation of concrescence: each prehension in any incomplete phase has being for every prehension in every later phase (and for the completed actual entity). Therefore, if one prehension can concresce into another prehension, then the one prehension is synontic to the other prehension. Thus concrescence is a special relation between prehensions which synonty underlies.

Whitehead holds an "epochal theory of time" (*PR* 105). According to this theory, the process of coming into being (i.e., "becoming") is "atomic" (*PR* 53). More precisely, an "act of becoming" is not indefinitely divisible into component acts of becoming such that each component act of becoming is either "earlier" or "later" than each other component act of becoming; thus there must be "atomic" acts of becoming which are ("temporally") indivisible (see his solution to Zeno's "Arrow" paradox [*PR* 105–107]). Are these "atomic" acts of becoming the finite actual entities (cf. *PR* 53)? How, then, can a finite actual entity be "divisible" into a succession of phases of concrescence? The process of coming into being must be "atomic" because each act of becoming must have an "immediate successor" (*PR* 107) (otherwise that act of becoming could not be succeeded by another act of becoming [*PR* 106]). Now the initial phase of simple physical feelings has an immediate successor, namely, the first supplementary phase of conceptual prehensions; in general, each incomplete phase has an immediate successor, namely, the immediately succeeding incomplete phase (or the final phase) (*PR* 327). Moreover, the becoming of a phase is nothing but the becoming of the prehensions in the phase. Thus each prehension is an "atomic" act of becoming (*PR* 354) which (since becoming [time] is not "uniquely serial" [*PR* 52]) has many immediate successors, namely, the prehensions which come into being in the immediately succeeding phase (or the completed actual entity). In short, both prehensions and finite actual entities (as completed unities of feeling) are "atomic" acts of becoming.[4]

8. *The Mutual Sensitivity of Subjective Forms*

Nonetheless, because of an actual entity's "subjective unity", its prehensions cannot be "abstracted" from it (*PR* 28–29, 338–339, 434). But the subjective unity presupposed by the prehensions which come into being in an incomplete phase (*PR* 39) is a unity of aim ("purpose"), namely, their "subjective aim" at concrescing into their "subject" actual entity (*PR* 339–340, 341–342). In particular, their subjective aim determines how they concresce by determining "how" they prehend that which they prehend (i.e., by determining their "subjective forms") (*PR* 28–29, 40–41, 355, 368, 369). Primarily because of its subjective form, a prehension cannot be "abstracted" from the actual entity into which it concresces (*PR* 29, 354). Therefore, paradoxically, although an actual entity is divisible into phases of prehensions, it is not ("temporally") divisible in respect of those prehensions' subjective forms (*PR* 108, 447).

A prehension has three "factors": its "subject" (the actual entity into which it concresces), its "datum" (that which it prehends), and its "subjective form" ("how" that which it prehends is prehended) (*PR* 35). Moreover, the "essential novelty" of a prehension is embodied in its subjective form (*PR* 354). But prehensions and subjective forms are registered as separate "Categories of Existence". If its subjective form is such an essential "factor" of a prehension, how can subjective forms and prehensions be separate basic types of entity?

Although Whitehead repudiates the Aristotelian doctrine of substance (*PR* 43–44), he retains an analogue of that doctrine in his explanation of the relation of prehensions to their subjective forms (*PR* 45, 354): Even though properties "inhere" in (and therefore are "dependent" in their mode of being on) substances, properties are distinguishable from substances. By analogy, even though subjective forms are essential "factors" of prehensions, subjective forms are distinguishable from prehensions. Accordingly, when we "abstract" its subjective form from a prehension, the only "remnant" of the subjective form is an eternal object (i.e., a "property") (*PR* 354, 356). When distinguished from prehensions, are subjective forms therefore nothing but eternal objects?

Subjective forms are of many types: "emotions, valuations, purposes, adversions, aversions, consciousness, etc." (*PR* 35). But they are all "emotional" (*PR* 246–248, 323–325, 356–358, 417–420) (where this metaphysical concept of emotion may be understood as an imaginative generalization of the concept of human emotion [*PR* 248]). In particular, any subjective form has two "factors" (*PR* 356): a "pattern of emotional quality" and a "pattern of emotional intensity" (*PR* 358). Now an emotion felt by a human being (e.g., he responds angrily) is distinguishable from the "universal" (the "property") exemplified in it (e.g., "angriness"). Accordingly, by analogy, a subjective form is distinguishable from the eternal object which has ingression into it. (Cf. also the distinction between a "color patch" and the color exemplified in the patch.) Therefore, when an eternal object (of the "subjective" species) ingresses into an actual entity to characterize "how" that actual entity prehends an entity, a subjective form comes into being (*PR* 33).

Because subjective forms are distinguishable from prehensions, the relations of subjective forms to one another are distinguishable from the relations of prehensions to one another. How, then, are subjective forms related to one another? Although subjective forms are distinguishable from eternal objects, we may understand the relations of subjective forms to one another in an actual entity by analogy with the relations of eternal objects to one another in the universe. Just as eternal objects "transcend" the creative advance of actual entities, so subjective forms "transcend" the phases of prehensions. Accordingly, just as each eternal object, because eternal, is always in being for every other, so each subjective form in a concrescence, because "nontemporal" (i.e., because of the "subjective unity" ("subjective aim") of that concrescence), comes into being "with" every other. Thus there is a universal relatedness of subjective forms in an actual entity that is analogous to the universal relatedness of eternal objects in the universe.

But subjective forms come into being in "phases" (*PR* 359). The subjective form of a simple physical feeling of a past actual entity is the "re-enaction" (the "reproduction") of the subjective form of the prehension by means of which the past actual entity is felt (*PR* 362–363, 364). The subjective form of a conceptual prehension of an eternal object (derived from a simple physical feeling of a past actual entity into which the eternal object has ingression) is a "valuation" of the eternal object (rather than a mere re-enaction of the past actual entity's valuation) (*PR* 367, 368, 380). The subjective form of an integral prehension is a "determination" of (i.e., an "elimination of indeterminations" in) the subjective forms of the prehensions integrated (such that the subjective forms of the prehensions integrated become components in the subjective form of the integral prehension) (*PR* 39, 131, 358, 359–360). For example, the subjective form of the simplest type of "physical purpose"— namely, an integral feeling integrated from a simple physical feeling and a conceptual feeling derived from the simple physical feeling— is the re-enacted subjective form of the simple physical feeling modified by the valuation of the conceptual feeling (*PR* 380). The subjective forms of all the prehensions, including the negative prehensions, in a concrescence contribute to the "emotional complex" which is the subjective form of the completed actual entity (*PR* 66, 359). In short, because an actual entity's prehensions concresce, the subjective forms of those prehensions also "grow together". Thus the "phases" of subjective forms are the phases of prehensions.

Nonetheless, subjective forms "transcend" the phases of concrescence. Even though the prehensions in an actual entity come into being in phases, the subjective forms of the prehensions are all "mutually sensitive" (*PR* 66, 292, 338, 359, 368–369, 420, 522). More precisely, because of the "subjective aim" motivating a concrescence of prehensions, the subjective form of each prehension is "mutually sensitive" with (is "determined" by, "adjusts" to, is in "pre-established harmony" with) the subjective form of every other prehension (*PR* 39, 40–41). In particular, because of the (aspect of the) subjective aim at "balanced intensity" (i.e., a maximal pattern of subjective intensities) in the subjective form of the completed actual entity, the subjective intensity in the subjective form of each prehension may be "heightened" or "attenuated" in relation to the subjective intensity in the subjective form of any other prehension (*PR* 41, 75, 424–427). For example, the intensity in the subjective form of a physical purpose is determined by the intensity in the subjective form of the conceptual feeling integrated into the physical purpose (*PR* 368); also, the intensity in the subjective form of the physical purpose may be adjusted because of the intensity in the subjective form of an intellectual feeling into which the physical purpose is integrated. Although divisible into phases of concrescence, an actual entity retains "subjective unity".

Thus the subjective forms in a concrescence are related to one another by means of the "relation of mutual sensitivity" (i.e., *x* is mutually sensitive with *y*). Just as each eternal object can be in a relation of patterning with or diversity from each other eternal object, so each subjective form in a concrescence is mutually sensitive with each other subjective form in the concrescence. Therefore, paradoxically, even though a prehension which comes into being in a later phase cannot concresce into a prehension which comes into being in an earlier phase, their subjective forms come into being "with" one another. Hence the very general meaning of the universal relation of synonty is disclosed in the special relation of mutual sensitivity: each subjective form in a concrescence has being for every other. Therefore, if one subjective form is mutually sensitive with another subjective form, then the one subjective form is synontic to the other subjective form. Thus mutual sensitivity is a special relation between subjective forms which synonty underlies.

The concrescence of prehensions is analogous to the creative advance of actual entities, and the mutual sensitivity of subjective forms is analogous to the relational essences of eternal objects. However, in contrast to eternal objects, subjective forms come into being (*PR* 33). How, then, can the successive becomings of prehensions be "transcended" by the becomings of their subjective forms? In stressing these analogies, have I split an actual entity into incompatible halves? (But cf. Whitehead's distinction between the "physical pole" and the "mental pole" of an actual entity [*PR* 380].)

Whitehead's theory of the internal process of concrescence is perhaps so intricate—or obscure—that it must always be problematical. However, it is evident that he intends a distinction between the multiplicity of prehensions into which an actual entity can be divided and the actual entity's subjective unity (*PR* 28–29). Accordingly, I intend, by extracting the relations of concrescence and mutual sensitivity, to make some sense of this distinction. But my aim is merely to define his "Categories of Existence" and not to elaborate fully every aspect of his metaphysics. Therefore, my interpretation of this theory must be somewhat arbitrary—especially the following imaginative generalization of the relation of mutual sensitivity.

Mutual sensitivity is a relation between the subjective forms in an actual entity, and concrescence is a relation between the prehensions. But how are subjective forms related to prehensions and prehensions to subjective forms? Each subjective form is the subjective form of some prehension. Accordingly, each subjective form in an actual entity is mutually sensitive with each prehension (in respect of its subjective form), and, conversely, each prehension (in respect of its subjective form) is mutually sensitive with each subjective form. Therefore, by imaginative generalization, mutual sensitivity is a special relation between the subjective forms and the prehensions in an actual entity (*PR* 420). (For convenience, the relation between a prehension and its own subjective form is incorporated in this imaginatively generalized relation of mutual sensitivity.) Just as each eternal object can ingress into each actual entity, so each subjective form in an actual entity is mutually sensitive with each prehension.

Concrescence is a relation between prehensions which come into being in different phases. In particular, an integral prehension which comes into being in an incomplete phase can only integrate prehensions which have already come into being in earlier phases. Thus prehensions which come into being in the same phase do not concresce into one another. How, then, are they related to one another? Just as the succession of phases of prehensions is analogous to the succession of actual entities, so a single phase of prehensions is analogous to a locus of contemporaneous actual entities (i.e., a "duration") (*PR* 188–192, 486–490). Accordingly, just as the actual entities in a duration are in a "unison of becoming" (*PR* 189–190, 192), so the prehensions in an incomplete phase come into being "with" one another. (However, this analogy is somewhat inappropriate, because contemporaneous actual entities are related to one another indirectly [see my Section 10].) In particular, in an incomplete phase each prehension must come into being "with" the other prehensions in such a manner as to be "integrable" with them in later phases

(*PR* 341). Therefore, by imaginative generalization, each prehension which comes into being in a particular incomplete phase is "mutually sensitive" with every other. Thus the prehensions which come into being in the same phase are related to one another by the imaginatively generalized relation of mutual sensitivity.

Prehensions concresce into an actual entity, and subjective forms are mutually sensitive with prehensions. But how are the subjective forms of the prehensions which concresce into an actual entity related to that actual entity? An actual entity, in the final phase of its concrescence, is "one complex, fully determinate feeling" (*PR* 38, 39) with a subjective form (*PR* 66, 359). Nonetheless, actual entities are distinguishable from prehensions (because an actual entity is "complete" whereas a prehension is "incomplete") (*PR* 28–29, 436–438). In order to reflect this analogy between actual entities and prehensions while maintaining the difference, I imaginatively generalize the relations of mutual sensitivity and concrescence as follows: The subjective forms of the prehensions which concresce into an actual entity are mutually sensitive with the actual entity's subjective form (because the actual entity's subjective form is distinguishable from the actual entity). But the subjective forms are not mutually sensitive with the actual entity itself (because the actual entity is "fully determinate"). Nonetheless, the subjective forms concresce into the actual entity (because they become components of the actual entity's subjective form). Finally, for convenience, the actual entity's subjective form concresces into the actual entity (because its subjective form is a "factor" of it).

Concrescence and mutual sensitivity, as imaginatively generalized, are special relations which the universal relation of synonty underlies. Each prehension in an incomplete phase can concresce into (and thus is synontic to) any prehension in any later phase; each prehension or subjective form concresces into (and thus is synontic to) an actual entity. Each subjective form in a concrescence is mutually sensitive with (and thus is synontic to) every other; each subjective form in a concrescence is mutually sensitive with (and thus is synontic to) each prehension, and each prehension is mutually sensitive with (and thus is synontic to) each subjective form; each prehension in an incomplete phase is mutually sensitive with (and thus is synontic to) every other. Thus the labyrinth of becomings in an internal process of concrescence conforms to a general pattern of interrelatedness definable by means of formal properties of synonty.

Prehensions concresce into an actual entity. More precisely, each prehension in an incomplete phase in the internal process of concrescence of an actual entity concresces into the completed actual entity in the final phase. But, according to Whitehead, an actual entity's "real internal constitution" is its whole internal process of concrescence (*PR* 37, 335). In distinguishing between prehensions and the actual entity into which they concresce, have I wrongly identified the actual entity with but one phase of its being? Just as a nexus is both a multiplicity (i.e., many actual entities prehending one another) and a "proper" entity (i.e., the unity emergent from those many actual entities' prehensions of one another), so an actual entity is both a multiplicity (in its succession of incomplete phases of prehensions) and a "proper" entity (as a completed unity of feeling emergent from the concrescence of those prehensions). (Also, an integral prehension in an incomplete phase is both a multiplicity [i.e., the succession of prehensions in earlier phases which are integrated together] and a "proper" entity [i.e., the one prehension emergent from the integration of those prehensions].) Therefore, whereas an actual entity comes into being as a multiplicity throughout its whole internal process of concrescence, it comes into being as a "proper" entity only in the final phase of its internal process of concrescence.

Although a multiplicity throughout its process of concrescence, an actual entity is more than an arbitrary aggregate. For it "inheres" in its process of concrescence as that at which its prehensions "aim" (*PR* 338–340, 341–344). Thus its many prehensions have a "subjective unity" provided by their "subjective aim" at producing it (as their "subject-superject").

But a subjective aim has "phases" (*PR* 75). For the subjective aim motivating the process of concrescence of an actual entity is successively modified in the succession of phases of prehensions (*PR* 342, 343). In the initial phase of the actual entity's concrescence, there is a ("hybrid") simple physical feeling of God's conceptual feeling of the eternal objects most relevant (according to his "valuation" of them) to the actual entity (*PR* 46, 343). In the first supplementary phase, there is a conceptual feeling, derived from the simple physical feeling, of the eternal objects felt by God (such that the subjective form of the conceptual feeling is the re-enaction of the subjective form of God's conceptual feeling) (*PR* 343). Thus the actual entity derives a conceptual feeling of subjective aim (i.e., its "initial subjective aim" or "initial aim") from God's "primordial nature"

(*PR* 343). This conceptual feeling of subjective aim derived from God is "simplified" in each succeeding supplementary phase by the elimination of "possibilities" ("alternatives") (i.e., eternal objects) felt by God (*PR* 342). In the final phase, the remaining eternal objects felt by the conceptual feeling of subjective aim have ingression into the datum of the complex unity of feeling which is the completed actual entity (such that they are components in contrasts providing balanced intensity of satisfaction) (*PR* 424–427).

But God is not a metaphysical principle invoked to explain what other metaphysical principles fail to explain. Instead, he is the "chief exemplification" of the metaphysical principles. Thus each finite actual entity in the actual world of an actual entity also motivates the process of concrescence of that actual entity. Let us consider, in particular, the actual entities in a "society". A society of actual entities is a nexus of actual entities which are ordered by their "genetic inheritance" (through their prehensions of one another) of a "defining characteristic" (an eternal object) (*PR* 50–51). The defining characteristic has ingression into each actual entity in the society; moreover, each actual entity in the society has a conceptual feeling of the defining characteristic (*PR* 50–51). Accordingly, there is genetic inheritance of the defining characteristic as follows: In the initial phase in the concrescence of an actual entity in the society, there are ("hybrid") simple physical feelings of some of the society's actual entities' conceptual feelings of the defining characteristic. In the first supplementary phase of the actual entity's concrescence, there are conceptual feelings, derived from the simple physical feelings, of the defining characteristic (*PR* 51). Thus each actual entity in a society derives conceptual feelings of its own defining characteristic from other actual entities in the society. In general, each finite actual entity in the actual world of an actual entity gives to that actual entity a selection of eternal objects that are relevant to its process of concrescence (*PR* 46).

Throughout its process of concrescence, an actual entity is a multiplicity of prehensions with a (subjective) unity of (subjective) aim. But the subjective aim derived from God is successively modified, and there are many other "aims" (motivations) derived from many other actual entities. Therefore, if the prehensions merely have a unity of aim, and since there are many aims (which, moreover, are successively modified), why are there not many unities? The subjective unity of the prehensions is grounded on the mutual sensitivity of the prehensions' subjective forms. For each subjective form is mutually sensitive with every other subjective form and with every prehension. Moreover, even when one prehension cannot concresce into another prehension, the one is mutually sensitive with some subjective form mutually sensitive with the other. Thus each prehension or subjective form in an actual entity is directly or indirectly mutually sensitive with every other. Therefore, since synonty underlies mutual sensitivity, each prehension or subjective form in an actual entity is directly or indirectly synontic to every other. (I term this relation of direct or indirect synonty between created mental entities [i.e., prehensions and subjective forms] "compresence" [see my Section 15].) Thus the multiplicity of prehensions and subjective forms which concresce into an actual entity, although not a "proper" entity, have the unity of a "cluster" (see my Section 15).

The prehensions and subjective forms which are involved in the concrescence of an actual entity are related to one another by means of the relations of concrescence and mutual sensitivity. But how are the "data" of prehensions related to one another?

9. *The Synthesis of Contrasts*

A prehension has as one of its "factors" its subjective form, and as another of its "factors" its "datum" (*PR* 35). Initially, the datum (or data) of one of an actual entity's prehensions is, according to the category of universal relativity, an entity (or multiplicity of entities) in the actual world of that actual entity (i.e., an entity [or multiplicity of entities] having the potentiality for being prehended by that actual entity). Subsequently, the process of prehending that initial datum (or data) results either in its *exclusion* (by a negative prehension) or in its *inclusion* (by a positive prehension). However, that which is "included" by a positive prehension is not the initial datum (or data) itself but only a "perspective" (*PR* 338). Therefore, a *positive* prehension (i.e., a "feeling") has as "factors" not only its subjective form and its initial data but also its "perspective" of those initial data, namely, its "objective datum" (*PR* 338). Whereas the initial data are entities (of any of the basic types) which are in the actual world of the prehending actual entity prior to the process of producing the positive prehension, the subjective form is produced by the process of producing the positive prehension (as a "record" of the "how" of the process), and, also, the objective datum is realized through the process of producing the positive prehension (as a "perspective" of the initial data). Thus both its subjective form and its objective datum are essential "factors" of a positive prehension. However, in contrast to subjective forms, which are registered in the "Categories of Existence" as a separate type of entity, "objective data" are not so registered, at least under that name. Are objective data and positive prehensions therefore indistinguishable?

The process of transition from initial data to objective datum is most clearly illustrated by the process whereby an actual entity produces one of its simple physical feelings: the initial datum is another actual entity (in the actual world of the first), and the objective datum is one of that other actual entity's prehensions. Consequently, both the initial data and the objective data of an actual entity's simple physical feelings are entities in that actual entity's actual world. In general, the objective data of an actual entity's positive prehensions are entities in that actual entity's actual world (*PR* 338). Therefore, even though they are essential "factors" of positive prehensions, both subjective forms and objective data are distinguishable from positive prehensions.

But this conclusion seems incompatible with the process of transition from initial data to objective datum whereby an actual entity produces one of its integral feelings. For the objective datum of an integral feeling is realized through the "synthesis" (*PR* 348) of the initial data of that feeling. How can the initial data of one of an actual entity's integral feelings be "synthesized" without imposing upon those data "relations" which are not to be found in that actual entity's actual world? (By analogy, according to a common interpretation of Kant's philosophy, empirical knowledge of physical objects is produced through a synthesis of a manifold of empirical intuition that imposes upon that manifold relations [of space, time, causality, etc.] not to be found in it.)

Such a synthesis of an objective datum from initial data is most clearly illustrated by the process whereby one actual entity integrates its simple physical feelings of other actual entities to produce a complex physical feeling of the nexus between those other actual entities. Perhaps the objective datum of the one actual entity's complex physical feeling is the nexus, and the initial data the other actual entities. In its "synthesis" of the nexus, does the one actual entity impose upon the other actual entities "relations" not to be found between them? The "relations" between the other actual entities that bind them together into a nexus are their prehensions of one another. The one actual entity, because it has a simple physical feeling of each of the other actual entities, feels the other actual entities' prehensions of one another. Consequently, by integrating its simple physical feelings of the other actual entities, the one actual entity "synthesizes" the other actual entities' prehensions of one another into a consistent objective datum (according to the "Category of Objective Identity" (*PR* 39, 347–348)). Therefore, although the objective datum of the one actual entity's complex physical feeling is the nexus, the initial data include, more accurately, the other actual entities' prehensions of one another. Hence the "relations" realized in the objective datum are already in the initial data. In summary, in its "synthesis" of a nexus, an actual entity does not impose but merely discloses "relations" between the actual entities in the nexus, namely, those actual entities' prehensions of one another.

Even though integral feelings of one type—complex physical feelings of nexūs—are distinguishable from their objective data, are integral feelings of the other type—integral feelings of "contrasts" (*PR* 348–350) so distinguishable? An integral feeling of a contrast is produced by integrating feelings of the entities to be "contrasted". Thus the objective datum of such an integral feeling is a contrast (i.e., a "synthesis") of entities (*PR* 33, 36), and the initial data the entities to be contrasted (i.e., synthesized). When entities are contrasted, they are set "side by side" so as to display particular relations between them (*PR* 348–349). (Thus the term "contrast" is misleading; when entities are "contrasted", they are both compared and contrasted; for example, Whitehead terms feelings of "generic contrasts" "comparative feelings" [*PR* 406].) Therefore, a contrast, although itself an entity realized through the synthesis of the entities contrasted, cannot be "abstracted" from the entities contrasted (*PR* 349). Does this synthesis of entities into a contrast impose upon those entities relations not to be found among them?

"Propositions" (*PR* 32) are the most prominent type of contrast (*PR* 36). Accordingly, the process of producing a "propositional feeling" (i.e., a positive prehension of a proposition) most clearly illustrates the process of producing an integral feeling of a contrast (*PR* 391–405). A propositional feeling is produced through the integration of a conceptual feeling and a physical feeling (*PR* 391–395). The objective datum of the propositional feeling is a proposition, and the initial data of the propositional feeling are the objective data of the conceptual feeling and the physical feeling, namely, an eternal object and either an actual entity (more accurately, one of that actual entity's prehensions) or a nexus (*PR* 393). The process of producing the propositional feeling synthesizes a "contrast" between the eternal object and the actual entity (or nexus). In particular, the actual entity (or nexus) is "contrasted" with the eternal object as an actual entity (or nexus) into which the eternal object *might* have ingression (*PR* 282, 398–399). The objective datum of the propositional feeling is therefore the "proposition" that the eternal object has the potentiality for ingression into the actual entity (or nexus). Thus the propositional feeling limits the eternal object's "pure (i.e., unlimited) potentiality" (*PR* 34) for ingression into any actual entity (or nexus) to a potentiality for ingression into this one particular actual entity (or nexus). Therefore, the relation realized in the objective datum—potentiality for ingression—was already a relation between the initial data. In summary, when a "subject" (an actual entity or nexus) and a "predicate" (an eternal object) are contrasted in a proposition, the relation of potentiality for ingression is not imposed upon but merely limited to that "subject" and "predicate".[5]

Even though one actual entity does not *impose* the relation of potentiality for ingression on another actual entity (or nexus) and an eternal object when it produces a propositional feeling of the proposition that the eternal object has the potentiality for ingressing into the other actual entity (or the nexus), the one actual entity thereby *limits* the relation of potentiality for ingression to the other actual entity (or the nexus) and the eternal object. What, then, is the significance of this "limitation"? The other actual entity (or the nexus) and the eternal object are in the actual world of the one actual entity. But is the *proposition* that the eternal object has the potentiality for ingressing into the other actual entity (or the nexus) *itself* in the actual world of the one actual entity? The relation of potentiality for ingression can have as referent *any* eternal object and as relatum *any* actual entity (or nexus) in the actual world of the one actual entity (the category of universal relativity). Therefore, the other actual entity (or the nexus) and the eternal object are not in and of themselves determinable as the sole relatum and referent of the relation of potentiality for ingression. Thus there must be a "third thing"—the one actual entity (or its propositional feeling)—which determines the other actual entity (or the nexus) and the eternal object as the sole relatum and referent of the relation of potentiality for ingression (with respect to that propositional feeling). Consequently, without imposing the relation of potentiality for ingression on the other actual entity (or the nexus) and the eternal object, but merely by limiting it to them, the one actual entity *produces* (i.e., *creates*) the proposition that the eternal object has the potentiality for ingressing into the other actual entity (or the nexus) (*PR* 33). In summary, an actual entity, by producing a propositional feeling of a proposition, produces that proposition.

Propositions function as "lures for feeling" (*PR* 37). Most importantly, an actual entity's subjective aim is supposedly based on that actual entity's feeling of a proposition (*PR* 37). Now an actual entity's subjective aim governs the process of integrating the prehensions in each incomplete phase in that actual entity's internal process of concrescence. And an incomplete phase, according to Whitehead, "has the unity of a proposition" (*PR* 342–343). Does this mean that an incomplete phase *is* a proposition? More exactly, are the multiplicity of prehensions in an incomplete phase the "subject" and the eternal objects in the subjective aim the "predicate" of a proposition? If an incomplete phase in an actual entity's process of concrescence is a proposition, then that actual entity cannot feel that proposition, for the "subject" of a proposition felt by that actual entity must be another actual entity or a nexus in that actual entity's actual world. Therefore, Whitehead's statement that an incomplete phase "has the unity of a proposition" is misleading (or mistaken), for it does not categorize incomplete phases but rather explains their unity by an analogy: A proposition contrasts an actual entity (or a nexus) and an eternal object, and, by analogy, an incomplete phase "unifies" a multiplicity of prehensions and a subjective aim. Accordingly, a proposition that an eternal object has the potentiality for ingressing into an actual entity (or a nexus) is analogous to an incomplete phase in which a subjective aim has the potentiality for governing the concrescence of a multiplicity of prehensions. In short, an eternal object's "potentiality for ingression" is analogous to a subjective aim's "potentiality for realization". In conclusion, Whitehead's doctrine of propositions is relevant to his doctrine of subjective aim, but that relevance, because obscure, must be clarified.

Generalizing from the synthesis of propositions, an actual entity's synthesis of a contrast of entities does not impose but merely discloses relations among the entities contrasted. But an actual entity's synthesis of a contrast of entities also limits the disclosed relations to the entities contrasted. Therefore, an actual entity, by synthesizing a contrast of entities, produces (i.e., creates) that contrast of entities as a novel entity distinct from any of the entities in its actual world prior to its process of concrescence (*PR* 33, 335, 352). (By analogy, a human being focuses his attention on select entities in his field of consciousness and thereby produces novel "associations".) In summary, an actual entity, by producing an integral feeling of a contrast, produces that contrast.

A least composite contrast is a contrast of entities which are of any of the basic types except contrasts. For example, a proposition is a contrast of an eternal object and either an actual entity or a nexus. But there are also contrasts of contrasts (*PR* 33). For example, the objective datum of an "intellectual feeling" (*PR* 406), an integral feeling produced through the integration of an "indicative feeling" (a type of physical feeling) and a propositional feeling, is a contrast of an actual entity (or a nexus) and a proposition. But the initial data of an actual entity's prehensions are in that actual entity's actual world (the category of universal relativity). How, then, can a proposition, a contrast produced by one of an actual entity's propositional feelings, be an initial datum for one of that actual entity's more composite integral feelings? Although a contrast is produced by an actual entity's integral feeling of that contrast, paradoxically, that contrast is also in that actual entity's actual world. Nonetheless, a contrast produced by an actual entity's integral feeling, because produced by that integral feeling, is not in that actual entity's actual world prior to the commencement of that actual entity's internal process of concrescence. Therefore, a contrast "produced" by an actual entity's integral feeling is also "introduced" by that integral feeling into that actual entity's actual world. But nothing (i.e., no entity) is thereby "added" to (i.e., "thrown" into) that actual entity's actual world, for the contrasting of entities does not impose upon those entities relations not to be found among them. In summary, an actual entity, by producing an integral feeling of a contrast, produces that contrast "into" its actual world (without disturbing that actual world).

This account of integral feelings of contrasts must be qualified. Consider the following example. One actual entity produces a propositional feeling of the proposition that a particular eternal object has the potentiality for ingressing into a particular nexus, and thereby produces that proposition. Later, another actual entity (in the future of the one actual entity) produces a simple physical feeling of the one actual entity's propositional feeling of the proposition, and thereby (indirectly) feels the proposition. The other actual entity therefore does not produce the proposition but merely feels the proposition as produced by the one actual entity. In general, then, a particular contrast is produced by the first actual entity to feel it (*PR* 352). However, this proposition that the particular eternal object has the potentiality for ingressing into the particular nexus can, in a sense, be "re-produced" by the other actual entity. The other actual entity, by producing its own conceptual feeling of the eternal object and its own physical feeling of the nexus, and then by integrating those feelings together, can produce its own propositional feeling of a proposition that the eternal object has the potentiality for ingressing into the nexus. But the one actual entity's proposition and the other actual entity's proposition are separate entities. For a proposition is founded not only on the entities contrasted by it but also on the actual entity (or the propositional feeling) that produces it. In general, then, a contrast, although itself an entity produced by an actual entity's synthesis of the entities contrasted, cannot be "abstracted" either from the entities contrasted or from that actual entity (*PR* 349, 352).

Another qualification is necessary. When prehensions are integrated by an actual entity to produce an integral prehension, and, coordinately, when the subjective forms of the integrated prehensions are mutually determined by that actual entity to produce the subjective form of the integral prehension, the eternal objects which have ingression into the subjective forms of the integrated prehensions become components in a complex pattern (where that pattern together with the eternal objects which it patterns is itself a complex eternal object characterizing the "how" of the integral prehension). Because it ingresses into the subjective form of the integral prehension rather than the objective datum, this complex pattern of eternal objects cannot be a contrast of those eternal objects. Nevertheless, Whitehead sometimes uses the term "contrast" in a manner that suggests that a pattern of eternal objects in a subjective form is a contrast of those eternal objects (*PR* 174–176, 424). Although we might distinguish between "objective contrasts" (i.e., objective data of integral feelings [of contrasts]) and "subjective contrasts" (i.e., "contrasts" of eternal objects in the subjective forms of integral feelings), we need not, because a "contrast" of eternal objects in a subjective form is simply a pattern of those eternal objects. Thus I only use the term "contrast" to mean "the objective datum of an integral feeling (of a contrast)".

An actual entity's synthesis of entities into a contrast realizes a re-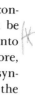
lation of "synthesis" (i.e., x is synthesized into y) between each of
the entities contrasted and the resultant contrast. This relation of
synthesis is comparable to the relation of concrescence (i.e., x concresces into y) between prehensions. Moreover, if an entity can be
synthesized into a contrast, then the entity has already come into
being (or is eternal) when the contrast comes into being. Therefore,
if an entity can be synthesized into a contrast, then the entity is synontic to the contrast. Thus synthesis is a special relation which the
universal relation of synonty underlies.

An actual entity's synthesis of entities into a contrast also realizes
a relation between the entities contrasted (i.e., x is contrasted with
y). However, whereas the relation of prehension between an entity
and an actual entity is a direct "seizing" or "grasping" of that entity
by that actual entity, this relation between contrasted entities is indirect. For entities are always contrasted by a "third thing"—an actual entity (integral feeling) that produces a contrast between those
entities. Therefore, this relation between contrasted entities is not a
special relation which synonty underlies. But contrasted entities
may nonetheless be related by a special relation which synonty underlies. For example, a nexus and an eternal object, when contrasted
in a proposition, are related by the relation of potentiality for ingression. However, contrasted entities need not be related by any
special relation which synonty underlies. In particular, when two
actual entities are contemporaneous, they are not related to one another by the relation of prehension (or by any other special relation
which synonty underlies), and yet they can be contrasted by a third
actual entity (in their future).

10. *Perception in the Mode of Presentational Immediacy*

But are contemporaneous actual entities only related indirectly? A
contemporary actual entity or nexus can be "perceived" in the
mode of "presentational immediacy" (*PR* 185). By "perception in
the mode of presentational immediacy" Whitehead usually means
(roughly) "conscious human perception of sense-data located in contemporary space" (*PR* 95–101). But the theory of presentational immediacy is also used to explain the concepts of rest and motion (*PR*
154–155, 191–192, 488–489, 492). Therefore, both human beings and

actual entities in relatively well-ordered societies (e.g., stones) have "perceptions" in the mode of presentational immediacy (see also *PR* 269–270, 478, 479, 484–485, 498). But human beings and their experiences are only analogous to actual entities and their prehensions. Thus the term "perception in the mode of presentational immediacy" is ambiguous: a human being's conscious perceptions in the mode of presentational immediacy must be distinguished from an actual entity's "perceptions" in the mode of presentational immediacy. And when applied to actual entities, the term "perception" must be understood as a metaphor (*PR* 361). Accordingly, an actual entity's "perceptions" in the mode of presentational immediacy are relatively complex integral prehensions produced in that actual entity's "higher phases of experience" (*PR* 406ff). In summary, "conscious human perception in the mode of presentational immediacy" is imaginatively generalized as "prehension in the mode of presentational immediacy".

But contemporaneous actual entities do not prehend one another (the category of universal relativity). How, then, can an actual entity "prehend" a contemporaneous actual entity "in the mode of presentational immediacy"? When a human being consciously perceives sense-data located in contemporary space, he does not consciously perceive the nexūs of actual entities located in the contemporary space. Therefore, he does not derive the sense-data from the contemporary nexūs (*PR* 95–101). Instead, he derives the sense-data from antecedent states of his own body (and from the antecedent world external to his body) (*PR* 179–184) and then "projects" the sense-data into the contemporary space (*PR* 262, 472–483, 491–496). Whitehead terms a human being's conscious perception of such derivation from the antecedent body (and world) "perception in the mode of causal efficacity (efficacy)" (*PR* 184). Thus presentational immediacy is grounded on causal efficacy (*PR* 179–182, 260–262, 475, 482). But a human being's "antecedent world" is, by analogy with an actual entity's actual world, the past, a past which he has in common with the contemporary nexūs. Thus the contemporary nexūs are also derivative from this "antecedent world". Therefore, the sense-data, derived from the common past, and "projected" into the contemporary space, "illustrate" (*PR* 474) the probable derivation of the contemporary nexūs from that common past. In summary, a human being's conscious perception of contemporary nexūs in the mode of presentational immediacy is indirect (*PR* 193, 256, 482–483).

By analogy, *"prehension* in the mode of presentational immediacy" means "an actual entity's prehension of eternal objects located in contemporaneous extensive regions". But the actual entity does not derive the eternal objects which it prehends as located in contemporaneous extensive regions from simple physical feelings of contemporaneous actual entities. Instead, just as the sense-data which the human being consciously perceives as located in contemporary space are derived from antecedent states of his body and "projected" into the contemporary space, so the eternal objects which the actual entity prehends as located in contemporaneous extensive regions are derived from prehensions in earlier phases of the actual entity's internal process of concrescence (*PR* 482) and "projected" into the contemporaneous extensive regions. And, just as the antecedent states of the human being's body are derivative from the antecedent world external to his body, so the prehensions in earlier phases of the actual entity's internal process of concrescence include simple physical feelings of actual entities in the actual entity's actual world. Thus "physical prehension" is an imaginative generalization of "conscious perception in the mode of causal efficacy". But the contemporaneous actual entities also have simple physical feelings of actual entities in their actual worlds. And, just as the human being and the contemporary nexūs are derivative from a common past, so the actual entity's actual world overlaps the actual worlds of the contemporaneous actual entities. Therefore, the eternal objects, derived from the actual entity's prehensions of its actual world, and "projected" into contemporaneous extensive regions, "illustrate" the probable derivation of the contemporaneous actual entities from their actual worlds. In summary, an actual entity's *prehension* of contemporaneous actual entities in the mode of presentational immediacy is indirect.

If prehension in the mode of presentational immediacy and conscious perception in the mode of presentational immediacy are distinguishable, why does Whitehead not distinguish them more clearly? When a human mind, a series of actual entities, has a conscious perception in the mode of presentational immediacy, that conscious perception endures through a multitude of those actual entities. Therefore, when a human mind has a conscious perception in the mode of presentational immediacy, each of the actual entities of that human mind through which that conscious perception endures has a *prehension* in the mode of presentational immediacy by means of which that conscious perception is sustained. In short, a conscious perception in the mode of presentational immediacy is derived from a series of prehensions in the mode of presentational immediacy.

Similarly, when a human mind has a conscious perception in the mode of *causal efficacy*, each of the actual entities of that human mind through which that conscious perception endures has a complex *physical* prehension by means of which that conscious perception is sustained. But conscious perception in the mode of causal efficacy, the foundation stone for Whitehead's attempt to refute Hume's theory of causality (*PR* 198–254), is also a source of evidence for the "reality" of causal relations. Thus the concept of conscious perception in the mode of causal efficacy not only is explained by the category of prehensions (together with other relevant categories) but also secures that category's applicability.

Prehension is a special relation which the universal relation of synonty underlies. Nonetheless, prehension in the mode of presentational immediacy, because it relates contemporaneous actual entities indirectly, is *not* a special relation which the universal relation of synonty underlies. How is this seeming contradiction to be resolved? The primary sense of "prehension" is a "seizing" or "grasping" which is "direct". In contrast, the sense of "prehension in the mode of presentational immediacy" is a "representing" or "inferring" which is "indirect". Therefore, if "prehension" is to have a mode of "presentational immediacy", the primary sense of "prehension" must be imaginatively generalized. Thus we must distinguish between the original relation of prehension, which is direct, and a generalized relation of prehension, which is either direct or indirect. Synonty underlies the original relation of prehension but not the generalized relation of prehension. (Accordingly, unless it is qualified by a phrase such as "in the mode of presentational immediacy" or some other context which indicates that it is to be understood in its generalized sense, the term "prehension" is always to be understood in its primary sense.)

The relation of prehension, when imaginatively generalized so as to be either direct or indirect, includes not only "prehension in the mode of presentational immediacy" but also, apparently, "anticipatory feeling". According to the "Category of Subjective Intensity" an actual entity has "anticipatory feelings" of actual entities in its future (*PR* 41, 424–425). But according to the category of universal relativity an actual entity only has feelings of actual entities in its past. How, then, are "anticipatory feelings" possible? The subjective aim governing an actual entity's internal process of concrescence not only is an aim at producing that actual entity but also is an aim at being effective in the internal process of concrescence of each actual entity in the "relevant future" (*PR* 41). In pursuing its aim at being effectively prehended by each relevant future actual entity, an actual entity apparently has an "anticipatory feeling" of its effects upon each relevant future actual entity. But how can an actual entity "feel" itself being felt? Whitehead's doctrine of "anticipatory feeling" is unusually cryptic. His few statements about "anticipatory feeling" are included in discussions of the "Category of Subjective Intensity" (but see *PR* 327–328). Therefore, an actual entity's "anticipatory feeling" might not be a feeling at all, not even in the generalized sense of "prehension", but might only be an aspect of that actual entity's subjective aim expressed in a manner quite misleading. Nonetheless, an alternative interpretation is suggested by my elaboration of "prehension in the mode of presentational immediacy". Just as "prehension in the mode of presentational immediacy" means "an actual entity's prehension of eternal objects located in *contemporaneous* extensive regions", so "anticipatory feeling" (more symmetrically, "prehension in the mode of anticipation") means "an actual entity's prehension of eternal objects located in *future* extensive regions". Therefore, in producing an "anticipatory feeling", an actual entity derives eternal objects from its prehensions of actual entities in its actual world and "projects" those eternal objects into future extensive regions in order to illustrate the probable derivation of future actual entities from their actual worlds (and, in particular, from that actual entity itself) (*PR* 103–104). In summary, "prehension in the mode of anticipation", as well as "prehension in the mode of presentational immediacy", is a relation between actual entities which is indirect. Thus prehension in the mode of anticipation is not a special relation which the universal relation of synonty underlies.

But my discussions of prehension in the mode of presentational immediacy and prehension in the mode of anticipation are seemingly ambiguous. (Since the two modes are similar, only presentational immediacy need be considered explicitly.) On the one hand, I state that "prehension in the mode of presentational immediacy" means "an actual entity's prehension of eternal objects located in contemporaneous extensive regions". On the other hand, I state that an actual entity's prehension of contemporaneous actual entities in the mode of presentational immediacy is indirect. Which, then does an actual entity prehend in the mode of presentational immediacy, eternal objects located in contemporaneous extensive regions or contemporaneous actual entities? An actual entity prehends, in the mode of presentational immediacy, *both* eternal objects located in contemporaneous extensive regions *and* contemporaneous actual entities, for the eternal objects illustrate the probable derivation of the contemporaneous actual entities from their actual worlds. More precisely, a prehension of contemporaneous actual entities in the mode of presentational immediacy is a complex integral prehension that includes, as prehensions integrated, conceptual feelings of illustrative eternal objects. Therefore, by directly prehending the illustrative eternal objects, the actual entity indirectly prehends the contemporaneous actual entities. Thus the indirectness of prehension in the mode of presentational immediacy is grounded on the directness of conceptual feeling.

However, when an actual entity directly prehends, in the mode of presentational immediacy, eternal objects located in contemporaneous extensive regions, it does not simply conceptually prehend the eternal objects. Instead, it directly prehends the eternal objects as located in the contemporaneous regions. Does it therefore prehend the contemporaneous regions directly? Some of Whitehead's remarks suggest that contemporaneous regions are prehended directly (in the mode of presentational immediacy) (*PR* 96, 188–189, 482, 484, 494). But these remarks seem incompatible with the category of universal relativity and the "ontological principle" (*PR* 36–37). According to the ontological principle, actual entities are the only "reasons"; therefore, regions are defined in terms of relations of extensive connection (i.e., extensive relations) among actual entities (and their prehensions and nexūs) (*PR* 103, 105, 118–119, 441). Therefore, an actual entity's prehensions of regions are derived from its prehensions of other actual entities. However, according to the category of universal relativity, an actual entity cannot prehend (in the primary sense of "prehension") contemporaneous actual entities. Therefore, it would seem that, according to the category of universal relativity and the ontological principle, an actual entity cannot prehend contemporaneous regions directly.

Nonetheless, according to the category of universal relativity, an actual entity can prehend (in the primary sense of "prehension") actual entities in its actual world (i.e., in its past). Therefore, according to the ontological principle, that actual entity can prehend extensive relations among those past actual entities (and their prehensions and nexūs). Consequently, that actual entity can prehend, in particular, the past regions which those past actual entities occupy. Now the extensive relations among (in particular, the regions occupied by) actual entities are definable in terms of the systematic scheme of extensive relations (*PR* 449–467). Thus the formal properties of extensive connection, which comprise the basis for the systematic scheme of extensive relations, must be ingredient in each actual entity (*PR* 440–441). But all possible extensive relations (in particular, all possible regions in the extensive continuum) are definable in terms of the formal properties of extensive connection. Therefore, when an actual entity prehends past actual entities, it can prehend all possible extensive relations (in particular, all possible subdivisions of the extensive continuum into regions). Therefore, when that actual entity prehends past actual entities, it can prehend, most particularly, the potentialities for subdivision into regions of that portion of the extensive continuum which is contemporaneous with it (*PR* 104). Thus contemporaneous regions, abstracted from the contemporaneous actual entities which occupy them, and existing as mere potentialities for occupation, can be prehended directly.

But contemporaneous actual entities occupy particular regions. How, then, can an actual entity distinguish the particular regions occupied by contémporaneous actual entities from all the other possible regions into which the contemporaneous portion of the extensive continuum can be subdivided? Because actual worlds overlap, an actual entity, by prehending its own actual world, can prehend the probable manner of derivation of contemporaneous actual entities from their actual worlds. Thus the actual entity can prehend the probable extensive relations of the contemporaneous actual entities (in particular, the approximate contemporaneous regions occupied by the contemporaneous actual entities). But Whitehead's explanation of how an actual entity determines the approximate contemporaneous regions occupied by contemporaneous actual entities contains technicalities which are most obscure (*PR* 472–483, 491–496) (but see *PR* 194). Nonetheless, for the sake of brevity, I must substitute a perhaps unsatisfactory sketch for the more thorough analysis which the subject requires. An actual entity can determine a contemporaneous region by "projection": A "strain" (or "strain-feeling") is a feeling whose objective datum importantly displays geometrical forms (e.g., points, straight lines, planes) (*PR* 472). The "seat" of a strain-feeling is a particular set of points in a particular region in the objective datum of the strain-feeling (*PR* 472). Straight lines, termed "projectors", are defined by pairs of points in the seat of a strain-feeling (*PR* 473, 476, 492, 493). Projectors, emanating from the seat of a strain-feeling, penetrate regions outside that seat; in particular, a "dense concurrence" of projectors may define a "focal region" outside that seat (*PR* 476, 492). (This theory of the "projective" determination of "focal" regions is apparently an imaginative generalization of the rudiments of projective geometry and geometric optics.) Now a prehension in the mode of presentational immediacy is a complex integral prehension that includes, as one of the prehensions integrated, a strain-feeling (*PR* 493). Therefore, when an actual entity prehends contemporaneous actual entities in the mode of presentational immediacy, the approximate contemporaneous regions occupied by the contemporaneous actual entities are focal regions of strain-feelings (*PR* 476–478, 482, 492, 493).

But an actual entity, when prehending in the mode of presentational immediacy, projects not only contemporaneous focal regions but also illustrative eternal objects, for the eternal objects are projected into the contemporaneous focal regions in order to illustrate the probable derivation of contemporaneous actual entities from their actual worlds. For example (and by analogy), the greyness of a stone, perceived by me now, illustrates the approximate region in contemporary space that is occupied by the actual entities which are the contemporary members of the society of actual entities which is the stone (*PR* 184–185). Therefore, by integrating a strain-feeling of a contemporaneous focal region with a conceptual feeling of an eternal object, an actual entity produces a prehension (in the mode of presentational immediacy) of the eternal object located in the contemporaneous focal region (*PR* 482, 493).

Nonetheless, when an actual entity directly prehends, in the mode of presentational immediacy, illustrative eternal objects located in contemporaneous focal regions, it only indirectly prehends the contemporaneous regions which the illustrated contemporaneous actual entities occupy. For the contemporaneous focal regions merely approximate to and therefore are distinct from the occupied contemporaneous regions (*PR* 261) (cf. the distinction between "strain-locus" and "presented duration" [*PR* 195–196, 488, 491–492]). Thus the indirectness of prehension in the mode of presentational immediacy is secured. Yet the contemporaneous focal regions and the occupied contemporaneous regions are subdivisions of one and the same extensive continuum, and, therefore, may overlap (or even coincide).

Hence the "space" of presentational immediacy is not "private". Therefore, although resembling "representationalist" theories of perception (e.g., Descartes's), Whitehead's doctrine of perception in the mode of presentational immediacy retains elements of the "direct realism" implicit in his earlier views on perception.[6]

Whitehead's doctrine of perception (prehension) in the mode of presentational immediacy seems inordinately complex. However, rather than an exhaustive analysis, the goal of my discussion is merely a demonstration that prehension in the mode of presentational immediacy is indirect. Therefore, for simplicity, I do not discuss several concepts which, although very relevant to his doctrine, are not very relevant to my limited goal. In particular, I do not discuss the relevance of "transmutation" (*PR* 98, 477), "physical purpose" (*PR* 482, 493), "propositional feeling" (*PR* 477), and "symbolic reference" (*PR* 262–263, 482).[7]

But why is Whitehead's doctrine of perception (prehension) in the mode of presentational immediacy so complex? His ostensible purpose in elaborating the doctrine is to buttress his critique of the philosophical orientation that makes epistemology primary (*PR* 54). But why should a critique of, for example, Hume's emphasis on sense perception and consequent scepticism about causality require the technicalities of the theory of the projective determination of focal regions? Whitehead's deeper purpose for such technicalities is to ground concepts expounded in his earlier writings on the philosophy of science, namely, *An Enquiry Concerning the Principles of Natural Knowledge* (*PNK*) and *The Concept of Nature* (*CN*) (see *PR* 191).[8] An event in nature which perceives simultaneous events is termed a "percipient event" (*PNK* 68). A complete whole of nature simultaneous with a percipient event is termed a "duration" (*PNK* 68). Although a percipient event is simultaneous with many durations, it is "cogredient" in the one duration containing the events which it perceives (*PNK* 70). Thus "cogredience" is to be understood in terms of "perception". In these earlier writings on the philosophy of science, Whitehead used two fundamental concepts —"cogredience" and "extension"—in order to analyze the spatiotemporal structure of events (including the concepts of "rest" and "motion") (*PNK* 202, *CN* 52). But he later discovered that another fundamental concept is necessary: "process" (*PNK* 202). In *Process and Reality,* where this concept of "process" is elaborated, the concept of "cogredience" is replaced by the concept of "prehension". Whereas cogredience is a relation of a percipient event to its present, prehension is a relation of an actual entity to its past. An actual entity is "contemporaneous" with another actual entity if neither prehends the other (*PR* 188). A locus of actual entities contemporaneous with an actual entity is termed a "duration". (More precisely, any two actual entities in a duration are contemporaneous, and, any actual entity outside that duration either is prehended by or prehends at least one actual entity in that duration [*PR* 487].) Although an actual entity is in many durations, it is "cogredient" in the one duration containing the actual entities which it prehends in the mode of presentational immediacy (*PR* 191).[9]

But the actual entities in a duration are in a "unison of becoming" (*PR* 189–190). For example, the particular actual entities in a particular duration which are also members of a particular society, because they are jointly responsible for the perpetuation of the society's defining characteristic, must be in a "unison of becoming". However, whereas prehensions which come into being in the same phase are mutually sensitive, actual entities which come into being in the same duration do not prehend one another, and, therefore, cannot be directly in a "unison of becoming". Thus a "unison of becoming" is not a "unity of becoming". Nonetheless, because any two actual entities which come into being in the same duration have actual worlds which overlap, they can be in a "unison of becoming" which is indirect. Therefore, when two actual entities are contemporaneous, neither is synontic to the other.

11. *Additional Special Relations*

Whitehead's basic types of entity—actual entities, prehensions, nexūs, subjective forms, eternal objects, and contrasts—are definable by means of formal properties of synonty (Chapter 3). Synonty, a universal relation implicit in his metaphysics, is disclosed by investigating special relations which it underlies—most importantly, prehension (Section 5), ingression (Section 5), patterning or diversity (Section 6), concrescence (Section 7), mutual sensitivity (Section 8), and synthesis (Section 9)—and special relations which it does not underlie—most importantly, prehension in the mode of presentational immediacy (Section 10).

Since synonty relates entities of each type to entities of every type, we must investigate special relations which it underlies that together can relate entities of each type to entities of every type. For one entity is synontic to another entity if and only if the one entity can have a special relation which synonty underlies to the other entity. But the special relations which synonty underlies that have already been investigated cannot together relate entities of each type to entities of every type. For example, one nexus is synontic to another nexus if and only if the one nexus can have a special relation which synonty underlies to the other nexus; but nexūs are not related to one another by any special relation that has already been investigated. Therefore, we must investigate additional special relations between entities.

Since there are six basic types of entity, we might investigate as many as 36 special relations. However, because of the importance of the special relations that have already been investigated, synonty has been disclosed sufficiently to warrant a more summary investigation of the special relations that remain. In particular, the remaining special relations are indicated by means of the partly arbitrary imaginative generalization of prehension and ingression.

Each eternal object can ingress into each actual entity. Each derivative created entity is derived from actual entities. Therefore, an eternal object, by ingressing into actual entities, "ingresses", in a generalized sense, into derivative created entities. For example, a society has a "defining characteristic" (i.e., an eternal object that ingresses into each of the actual entities in the society) (*PR* 50–51), and relations (eternal objects) are abstracted from contrasts (derivative created entities) (*PR* 349–350). However, an eternal object of the "objective" species cannot ingress (in the generalized sense) into the subjective form of a prehension (*PR* 445–446); nonetheless, because it "has being for" the subjective form of the prehension (for example, it can ingress into actual entities in the datum of the prehension), it must be excluded from having the potentiality for ingression (in the generalized sense) into the subjective form of the prehension. Therefore, each eternal object either can ingress (in the generalized sense) into or is excluded from having the potentiality for ingression (in the generalized sense) into each created entity (cf. patterning or diversity). For brevity, I symbolize the relation ingression (in the generalized sense) or exclusion from ingression (in the generalized sense) by the term "ingression$_*$". In short, ingression$_*$ is a special relation which synonty underlies. Thus each eternal object is synontic to each created entity.

Conversely, each actual entity can "be ingressed into" by each eternal object. Because each eternal object is "eternal", and, therefore, "transcends" the creative advance of actual entities, it is, in a sense, both in the past and in the future of each actual entity. Accordingly, when each actual entity comes into being, it "has being for" each eternal object, in that it was or might have been ingressed into by the eternal object. Hence the converse of ingression (i.e., ingression^{-1})—being ingressed into—relates actual entities to eternal objects. More generally, when each created entity comes into being, it "has being for" each eternal object, in that it was or might have been ingressed$_*$ into by the eternal object. Hence the converse of ingression$_*$ (i.e., ingression$_*$$^{-1}$) relates created entities to eternal objects. In short, ingression^{-1} and ingression$_*$$^{-1}$ are special relations which synonty underlies. Thus each created entity is synontic to each eternal object.

Each entity in the actual world of an actual entity can be prehended by the actual entity. Each entity in the actual world of the actual entity (except contrasts synthesized by the actual entity), because it has already come into being prior to the commencement of the actual entity's internal process of concrescence, "has being for" each of the actual entity's prehensions and subjective forms. Therefore, an entity in the actual world of the actual entity, in being prehended by the actual entity, is "prehended", in a generalized sense, by one of the actual entity's prehensions. For example, one of another actual entity's prehensions is positively prehended (in the generalized sense) by a simple physical feeling, an eternal object by a conceptual feeling, and a nexus or contrast by an integral feeling. Moreover, an entity in the actual world of the actual entity, in being prehended (in the generalized sense) by one of the actual entity's prehensions, "affects" (and, therefore, is prehended, in the generalized sense, by) the subjective form of the prehension (*PR* 356). For example, when one of another actual entity's prehensions is positively prehended (in the generalized sense) by a simple physical feeling, the subjective form of the prehension is "re-enacted" by the subjective form of the simple physical feeling (*PR* 362). However, a nexus in the actual world of the actual entity cannot be prehended (in the generalized sense) by any of the actual entity's simple physical feelings; nonetheless, because it has already come into being for the actual entity, it must be excluded from having the potentiality for being prehended (in the generalized sense) by the simple physical feelings. Consequently, by imaginative generalization, each entity in the actual world of an actual entity (except contrasts synthesized by that actual entity) can be prehended (in the generalized sense) by or is excluded from having the potentiality for being prehended (in the generalized sense) by each of the actual entity's prehensions and subjective forms. For brevity, I symbolize the relation prehension (in the generalized sense) or exclusion from prehension (in the generalized sense) by the term "prehension$_*$". In short, prehension$_*$ is a special relation which synonty underlies. Thus each entity in the actual world of an actual entity (except contrasts synthesized by the actual entity) is synontic to each of the actual entity's prehensions and subjective forms.

A nexus is a multiplicity of actual entities interrelated by their prehensions of one another. Hence a nexus comes into being when the actual entities in the nexus come into being. Accordingly, in order that a nexus can be prehended by an actual entity, each actual entity in the nexus must be prehended by the actual entity. Since synonty underlies prehension, when a nexus is synontic to an actual entity, each actual entity in the nexus is synontic to the actual entity. Therefore, by imaginative generalization, a nexus is synontic to an entity of any type if and only if each actual entity in the nexus is synontic to the entity.

Conversely, when an entity of any type can be prehended by each actual entity in a nexus, then it "has being for" the nexus as a whole, and, therefore, by imaginative generalization, can be prehended$_*$ by the nexus. However, if an actual entity in a nexus is prehended by every other actual entity in the nexus, then any one of the actual entity's prehensions, because it concresces into the actual entity, is synontic to every actual entity in the nexus, and yet cannot be prehended$_*$ by the nexus; for the actual entity into which it concresces cannot be prehended$_*$ by the nexus, because an actual entity cannot prehend itself. Therefore, an entity of any type is synontic to a nexus if and only if it is synontic to each actual entity in the nexus (but cannot concresce into any).

Thus one nexus is synontic to another nexus if and only if each actual entity in the one is prehended by every actual entity in the other. However, one nexus is, in a sense, related to another nexus when some actual entities in the one are prehended by some actual entities in the other and some actual entities in the other are prehended by some actual entities in the one (i.e., when the nexūs are contemporaneous). Nonetheless, the actual entities in the one which are prehended by the actual entities in the other are themselves in a nexus (a nexus which is a component of the one); the actual entities in the other which prehend the actual entities in the one are themselves in a nexus (a nexus which is a component of the other); etc. Hence the contemporaneous nexūs are related to one another in that a component nexus of the one is synontic to a component nexus of the other and a component nexus of the other is synontic to a component nexus of the one. Thus contemporaneous nexūs are related "indirectly".

According to the category of universal relativity, each entity in the actual world of an actual entity can be prehended by the actual entity. Analogously, by imaginative generalization, each entity in the actual world of an actual entity (except contrasts synthesized by the actual entity) can be prehended$_*$ by the prehensions and subjective forms which are the components of the actual entity and by some of the nexūs in which the actual entity is a component.

Although synonty underlies prehension (i.e., x is prehended by y), it does not underlie the converse of prehension (i.e., x prehends y). For an actual entity has not already come into being when the created entities in its actual world come into being. Thus an actual entity is not synontic to any created entity in its actual world. Moreover, synonty does not underlie the converse of prehension$_*$. For, when a created entity has not yet come into being, it is "indeterminate", and thus does not "have being for" entities which have already come into being. Thus a created entity derived from an actual entity (or actual entities) is not synontic to any created entity in the actual world (or actual worlds) of the actual entity (or actual entities) (except some contrasts synthesized by the actual entity are synontic to others). In short, the future is indeterminate.

Synonty underlies ingression$_*$, ingression^{-1}, ingression$_*^{-1}$, and prehension$_*$. Ingression$_*$, ingression^{-1}, ingression$_*^{-1}$, and prehension$_*$ underlie the special relations which synonty underlies that have not already been investigated. For example, "re-enaction" is a relation between subjective forms in diverse actual entities; since synonty underlies prehension$_*$ and prehension$_*$ underlies re-enaction, synonty underlies re-enaction. Therefore, by means of the imaginative generalization of prehension and ingression, the remaining special relations which synonty underlies are indicated.

The special relations which synonty underlies that together can relate entities of each type to entities of every type—prehension, ingression, patterning or diversity, concrescence, mutual sensitivity, synthesis, ingression$_*$, ingression^{-1}, ingression$_*^{-1}$, and prehension$_*$—are summarized in the following chart:

the relata of synonty

	actual entities	prehensions	nexūs	subjective forms	eternal objects	contrasts
actual entities	prehension	prehension$_*$	prehension$_*$	prehension$_*$	ingression^{-1}	synthesis
prehensions	prehension concrescence	concrescence mutual sensitivity prehension$_*$	prehension$_*$	mutual sensitivity prehension$_*$	ingression$_*^{-1}$	synthesis
nexūs	prehension	prehension$_*$	prehension$_*$	prehension$_*$	ingression$_*^{-1}$	synthesis
subjective forms	prehension concrescence	mutual sensitivity prehension$_*$	prehension$_*$	mutual sensitivity prehension$_*$	ingression$_*^{-1}$	synthesis
eternal objects	ingression prehension	ingression$_*$ prehension$_*$	ingression$_*$ prehension$_*$	ingression$_*$ prehension$_*$	patterning diversity	synthesis ingression$_*$
contrasts	prehension	prehension$_*$	prehension$_*$	prehension$_*$	ingression$_*^{-1}$	synthesis

the referents of synonty

12. *The Universal Relation of Synonty*

According to the "Category of the Ultimate", when one actual entity comes into being from the many entities in its actual world, the many are "together" in the one (*PR* 32). In particular, the many entities in its actual world are "together" with (i.e., prehended by) the one actual entity, eternal objects are "together" with (i.e., ingress into) the one actual entity, the eternal objects which ingress into the one actual entity are "together" (i.e., in relations of patterning or diversity) with one another in the one actual entity, prehensions of the many entities in its actual world are "together" (i.e., in relations of concrescence or mutual sensitivity) with one another in the one actual entity, etc. Synonty, the universal relation of "togetherness" between entities, underlies these special relations of "togetherness" (cf. *PR* 32). Thus the meaning of synonty is prefigured in the "Category of the Ultimate".

Creativity is, according to the "Category of the Ultimate", the "ultimate principle" exemplified in the coming into being of one actual entity from the many entities in its actual world (*PR* 31). Moreover, the coming into being (i.e., "becoming") of the one actual entity is the creation (i.e., "creative advance") of a "novel" entity (i.e., an entity in addition to the many entities in its actual world) (*PR* 31–32). Consequently, before the one actual entity comes into being, it is not in being, and, therefore, does not "have being for" (i.e., is not synontic to) any created entity in its actual world. Thus the indeterminateness of the future is implicit in the principle of creativity.

My aim is to define Whitehead's basic types of entity by means of formal properties of synonty. Synonty is a "universal" relation, because it underlies special relations that together can relate entities of each type to entities of every type. However, it is not (coextensive with) "the universal relation", because it does not relate each entity to every entity. In particular, it does not relate any actual entity to the created entities in the actual entity's actual world (i.e., it does not underlie the converse of prehension), because each actual entity exemplifies the principle of creativity. If it were to relate each entity to every entity, then the entities of any one type could not be distinguished from the entities of any other type by means of its formal properties. Therefore, it has formal properties by means of which the basic types are definable because, even though it relates entities of each type to entities of every type, there are entities between which it does not hold.

When an actual entity comes into being, is is "*self*-creative" (*PR* 38). After an "initial phase" "determined" by a "public" actual world, its coming into being is "private", its self-creation "free". Therefore, while it comes into being, if another actual entity comes into being, the two are not "together" (i.e., neither prehends the other). The coming into being of two contemporaneous actual entities is a "unison of becoming" not a "unity of becoming". Accordingly, in addition to not underlying the converse of prehension, synonty does not underlie prehension in the mode of presentational immediacy. Thus synonty does not relate actual entities which are contemporaneous.

Just as one actual entity comes into being from the many entities in its actual world, a prehension not in the initial phase comes into being from prehensions in earlier phases. Furthermore, the coming into being of the prehension is the creation of a "novel" entity (i.e., an entity in addition to the prehensions in the earlier phases). Hence, before the prehension comes into being, it is not in being, and does not "have being for" any prehension in an earlier phase. Thus synonty does not relate any one of an actual entity's prehensions to any of the actual entity's prehensions which have already come into being in earlier phases of concrescence. In short, synonty does not underlie the converse of concrescence.

By imaginative generalization, creativity is the ultimate principle exemplified in the coming into being of one created entity (i.e., actual entity, prehension, nexus, subjective form, or contrast) from the many entities which have already come into being or are always in being (*PR* 33). Accordingly, before a created entity comes into being, it is not in being, and, therefore, does not "have being for" any created entity which has already come into being. In short, the principle of creativity grounds the indeterminateness of "later" stages of process. Thus synonty does not underlie the converses of prehension, concrescence, synthesis, and prehension$_*$.

Each of an actual entity's subjective forms comes into being "with" (i.e., is mutually sensitive with) every other of its subjective forms and all of its prehensions, and each prehension in a particular phase comes into being "with" (i.e., is mutually sensitive with) every other prehension in the phase. Thus there are created entities "together" in one actual entity such that each is synonic to every other (for synony underlies the converse of mutual sensitivity). However, given two created entities which are not mutually sensitive, if one comes into being while the other comes into being, then the two are not "together" (i.e., neither is synonic to the other). In other words, by imaginative generalization, two created entities are "contemporaneous" if and only if neither is synonic to the other. Thus synony does not relate created entities which are contemporaneous (i.e., it does not underlie "prehension$_*$ in the mode of presentational immediacy").

Because actual entities, prehensions, nexūs, subjective forms, and contrasts all "come into being", there are entities between which synony does not hold. In particular, there are two forms of "nonsynonty" between different entities: One created entity is synonic to another but the other is not synonic to the one (the generalization of "creative advance"). One created entity is not synonic to another and the other is not synonic to the one (the generalization of "unison of becoming"). Thus the "Category of the Ultimate", the category "presupposed" by every other category, grounds my definitions of Whitehead's "Categories of Existence".

Becoming is, in a sense, a universal "property" of created entities. However, a created entity does not come into being simpliciter. Instead, the coming into being of a created entity is a "creative advance" conditioned by other created entities and conditioning other created entities. For example, an actual entity comes into being from its actual world and for its future, and a subjective form comes into being with other subjective forms. Accordingly, becoming is, more appropriately, a relation between a created entity and another entity (i.e., x comes into being for y). In particular, there are two modes of becoming between different entities: One created entity has already come into being for another entity (prehension, concrescence, synthesis, ingression^{-1}, ingression$_*^{-1}$, prehension$_*$). One created entity comes into being with another created entity (mutual sensitivity).

Whereas created entities come into being, eternal objects, because "eternal" (i.e., always in being), do not. However, an eternal object is not "always in being" simpliciter. Instead, an eternal object is a "form of definiteness" for actual entities. Accordingly, "eternality" is, more appropriately, a relation between an eternal object and another entity (i.e., x is always in being for y). There is just one mode of eternality: One enternal object is always in being for another entity (ingression, patterning or diversity, ingression$_*$).

One entity is synontic to another entity when, roughly, the one "has being for" the other. One entity is not synontic to another entity when, roughly, the one "does not have being for" the other. Accordingly, there are three modes of synonty—the two modes of becoming and the one mode of eternality—and two modes of nonsynonty: One entity is synontic to (i.e., has being for) another entity if and only if either the one has already come into being for the other (prehension, concrescence, synthesis, ingression^{-1}, ingression$_*^{-1}$, prehension$_*$) or the one is always in being for the other (ingression, patterning or diversity, ingression$_*$) or the one comes into being with the other (mutual sensitivity). One entity is not synontic to (i.e., does not have being for) another entity if and only if either the one has not yet come into being for the other (the converses of prehension, concrescence, synthesis, and prehension$_*$) or the one comes into being independently of the other (contemporaneity). Thus the meaning of synonty is disclosed by investigating the special relations which synonty underlies and the special relations which synonty does not underlie.

My aim is not to analyze the meaning of synonty but rather to define types of entity by means of synonty's formal properties. Thus the meaning of synonty is only disclosed sufficiently to make my definitions meaningful. For my definitions of the primary dichotomies and basic types have the following form: An entity is of such and such a type if and only if it satisfies a condition involving synonty (or already defined types or relations).

For the sake of clarity, I express each definition both informally and abbreviately. In order to abbreviate the informal expression of a definition, I use the standard logical signs of modern symbolic logic together with artificial descriptive signs for synonty and the various types of entity (and relations) defined by means of synonty. However, the abbreviate expression of a definition is not a "formalization"; hence there is no problem of "interpreting" "undefined" signs. In particular, I use "$x \rightarrow y$" as an artificial sign for the relation x is synontic to y (where the "$\rightarrow$" pictures that an actual entity is the "consequent" of the entities in its actual world). In addition, I use a capital letter or letters for each type of entity (the letter(s) being taken from the standard term for the type), for example, "E" for eternal entities, "SF" for subjective forms. Accordingly, abbreviate expression of definitions of primary dichotomies and basic types have the form

$$(x)(Tx \equiv \ldots x \ldots) \qquad\qquad Do$$

where the definiens "$\ldots x \ldots$" only contains logical signs, the artificial sign for synonty, or artificial signs for types of entity (or relations) already defined by means of synonty. Thus the definiens "$\ldots x \ldots$" expresses a condition involving synonty (or already defined types or relations) that divides the universe of entities into two "segments", namely, those entities which satisfy the variable "x" and those entities which do not.

In addition to using "explicit" definitions to define the primary dichotomies and basic types, I use "implicit" definitions (e.g., equivalence relation definitions) to define particular "multiplicities" of entities—most importantly, "clusters" (Section 15) and "durations" (Section 16). However, these definitions of multiplicities, and also other consequences which I derive from the formal properties of synonty, are ancillary to the definitions of types of entity.

In summary, by investigating special relations which it underlies —prehension, ingression, patterning or diversity (and its converse), concrescence, mutual sensitivity (and its converse), synthesis, ingression$_*$, ingression^{-1}, ingression$_*^{-1}$, and prehension$_*$—and special relations which it does not underlie—prehension in the mode of presentational immediacy, the converses of prehension, concrescence, synthesis, and prehension$_*$, and contemporaneity—the universal relation of synonty is disclosed.

3

Types of Entity

13. *Finite and Infinite*

My aim is to divide the entities of Whitehead's ontology into primary dichotomies and basic types by means of formal properties of synonty. Which, then, are the relevant formal properties?

We may distinguish sixteen elementary formal properties of relations: reflexiveness, symmetry, transitivity, connectedness (the "positive" properties); irreflexiveness, asymmetry, intransitivity, disconnectedness (the contraries of the "positive" properties); nonreflexiveness, nonsymmetry, nontransitivity, nonconnectedness (the contradictories of the "positive" properties); nonirreflexiveness, nonasymmetry, nonintransitivity, nondisconnectedness (the contradictories of the contraries of the "positive" properties). Whereas more "standard" relations are more readily classifiable in terms of these formal properties (in particular, an equivalence relation is reflexive, symmetric, and transitive, and a serial relation is irreflexive, transitive, and connected), synonty is nonreflexive, nonirreflexive, nonsymmetric, nonasymmetric, nontransitive, nonintransitive, nonconnected, and nondisconnected.

Yet the very general meaning of synonty—that x is synontic to y when x has being for y—suggests that synonty is reflexive. For surely an entity has being for itself. (A relation is reflexive when each relatum has the relation to itself; a relation is irreflexive when no relatum has the relation to itself.) But an actual entity cannot prehend itself (*PR* 130). For it cannot prehend an entity which has not already come into being. Therefore, since synonty underlies prehension (and since an actual entity has no other special relation which synonty underlies to itself), an actual entity is not synontic to itself. Thus synonty is nonreflexive.

But an actual entity is "actual" because it is "self-functioning" (*PR* 38). Is the self-functioning of an actual entity a special relation (of that actual entity to itself) which synonty underlies? An actual entity is self-functioning because it is the "aim" of an internal process involving the concrescence of prehensions. It cannot come into being through the concrescence of components which include itself. For it is not already in being while it comes into being. Thus an actual entity as aim is "mediately" related to itself as product ("satisfaction") through the process of concrescence of its prehensions. Self-functioning, apparently the immediate relation of a single entity to itself, is really derived from the immediate relation of many entities to one another.

Even though an actual entity, because it is not already in being while it comes into being, does not have being for itself, does an eternal object, because it is always in being, have being for itself? But a pattern cannot be a component of itself. For eternal objects are ordered by the relation of patterning into "hierarchies" (cf. *Science and the Modern World,* pp. 167ff). (Analogously, in Whitehead's *Principia Mathematica* functions are ordered in a hierarchy [of logical types].) Consequently, a pattern cannot have a relation of diversity to itself. For the "relational essence" of a pattern excludes as components only those eternal objects which could be components if not excluded. Therefore, since synonty underlies patterning or diversity (and since an eternal object has no other special relation which synonty underlies to itself), an eternal object is not synontic to itself.

Actual entities and eternal objects are the most fundamental types of entity in Whitehead's ontology (*PR* 37). Accordingly, the creative advance of actual entities (the irreflexiveness of prehension and concrescence) and the hierarchical ordering of eternal objects (the irreflexiveness of patterning) suggest a generalization: no entity of any type is related to itself by any special relation which synonty underlies. Perhaps, then, synonty is irreflexive.

But this imaginative generalization of irreflexiveness is somewhat arbitrary. For example, a nexus is, in a sense, related to itself, since the actual entities in the nexus prehend one another. Nonetheless, a nexus is synontic to an entity when every actual entity in the nexus is synontic to the entity, and, an entity is synontic to a nexus when the entity can be prehended by every actual entity in the nexus. Therefore, because each actual entity in a nexus cannot be prehended by every actual entity in the nexus (for example, an actual entity cannot prehend itself), a nexus is not synontic to itself.

Moreover, no entity of any other basic type is synontic to itself. A prehension cannot come into being through the concrescence of components which include itself, because it is not already in being while it comes into being. Also, somewhat arbitrarily, a prehension or a subjective form cannot be mutually sensitive to itself. A contrast cannot be a component of itself, since it comes into being through a synthesis of entities which have already come into being. Apparently, then, no entity of any basic type is synontic to itself. Hence an imaginative generalization of irreflexiveness, although somewhat arbitrary, is not incoherent.

But synonty is *not* irreflexive. There is a counterexample in Whitehead's metaphysics: God. For God, an actual entity, can prehend himself. God prehends each finite actual entity (by his "consequent nature") and is prehended by each finite actual entity (by his "superjective nature") (*PR* 134–135, 532). A finite actual entity prehends God by means of a hybrid (simple) physical feeling (and thereby derives its initial subjective aim) (*PR* 343–344). Since the objective datum of an actual entity's simple physical feeling of another actual entity is one of the other actual entity's prehensions, the objective datum of God's simple physical feeling of a finite actual entity is one of the finite actual entity's prehensions. Therefore, God can feel, in particular, a finite actual entity's hybrid (simple) physical feeling of himself. Thus God can prehend himself. Hence synonty is both nonreflexive and nonirreflexive.

God is synontic to himself, whereas every other entity is not synontic to itself. Thus synonty, although nonreflexive and nonirreflexive among entities generally, is reflexive among "infinite" entities and irreflexive among "finite" entities. Accordingly, I define infinite entities and finite entities as follows: An entity is infinite if and only if it is synontic to itself (*D1*). An entity is finite if and only if it is not synontic to itself (*D2*). Abbreviating "infinite" as "*I*" and "finite" as "*F*", these definitions are abbreviated as follows:

$$(x)(Ix \equiv x \rightarrow x) \qquad\qquad D1$$
$$(x)(Fx \equiv {\sim}x \rightarrow x) \qquad\qquad D2$$

This division of entities into finite and infinite is a dichotomy: An entity is finite if and only if it is not infinite (*T1*):

$$(x)(Fx \equiv {\sim}Ix) \qquad\qquad T1$$

Thus the entities of Whitehead's ontology are divisible into the primary dichotomy of finite entities and infinite entities by means of formal properties of synonty.

14. *Created and Eternal*

The meaning of synonty—that x is synontic to y when x has being for y—also suggests that synonty is symmetric: When one entity has being for another entity, then the other entity is surely in being (and therefore has being for the one entity). (A relation Rxy is symmetric when

$$(x)(y)(Rxy \supset Ryx)$$

and asymmetric when

$$(x)(y)(Rxy \supset {\sim}Ryx).)$$

But a finite actual entity is not "in being" simpliciter; instead, it "comes into being" (i.e., is "created") by an internal process of concrescence. In particular, when it comes into being, it prehends each finite actual entity which has already come into being, but no finite actual entity which has not yet come into being. For the future is indeterminate. Accordingly, since synonty underlies prehension (and since finite actual entities have no other special relation which synonty underlies to one another), when one finite actual entity is synontic to another finite actual entity, then the other finite actual entity is not synontic to the one finite actual entity. Thus synonty is nonsymmetric (i.e.,

$$(\exists x)(\exists y)(x \to y \cdot {\sim}y \to x)$$

where x and y are finite actual entities).

Although nonsymmetric, synonty is not asymmetric. God, because he is always in being, is "eternal" (and "everlasting") (PR 524–525). Thus God is prehended by each finite actual entity and each finite actual entity is prehended by God. Moreover, each prehension, nexus, subjective form, eternal object, and contrast can be prehended by God; conversely, God can have a special relation which synonty underlies to each prehension, nexus, subjective form, eternal object, and contrast. And God can prehend himself. Thus God is synontic to every entity and every entity is synontic to God. Hence synonty is both nonsymmetric and nonasymmetric.

Eternal objects are also eternal (i.e., always in being). Each eternal object can have a relation of patterning with or diversity from each other eternal object. Each eternal object can ingress into each actual entity (and, by imaginative generalization, can ingress$_*$ into each prehension, nexus, subjective form, and contrast). And, conversely, each actual entity, prehension, nexus, subjective form, and contrast can be ingressed$_*$ into by each eternal object. But an eternal object is not synontic to itself. Thus each eternal object is synontic to every other entity and every other entity is synontic to it. In general, each eternal entity (i.e., eternal object or God) is synontic to every other entity and every other entity is synontic to it. Thus synonty is symmetric between eternal entities and entities generally.

A prehension, nexus, subjective form, or contrast comes into being (i.e., is created) when the actual entity (or actual entities) from which it is derived comes into being. In general, then, when a created entity (i.e., a finite actual entity, prehension, nexus, subjective form, or contrast) comes into being, it is not synontic to any created entity which has already come into being, but every created entity which has already come into being is synontic to it. For the future is indeterminate for every entity which comes into being. Thus synonty is nonsymmetric among created entities.

Eternal objects and God, because they are always in being, are synontic to (almost) every entity, whereas finite actual entities, prehensions, nexus, subjective forms, and contrasts, because they come into being, are not synontic to past entities. Thus synonty, although nonsymmetric and nonasymmetric among entities generally, is symmetric between eternal entities and entities generally and nonsymmetric among created entities. Accordingly, I define eternal entities and created entities as follows: An entity is eternal if and only if it is synontic to every other entity and every other entity is synontic to it (D3). An entity is created if and only if it is not synontic to some other entity or some other entity is not synontic to it (D4). Abbreviating "eternal" as "*E*" and "created" as "*C*", these definitions are abbreviated as follows:

$$(x)[Ex \equiv (y)(x \neq y \supset \cdot x \to y \cdot y \to x)] \qquad D3$$
$$(x)\{Cx \equiv (\exists y)[x \neq y \cdot (\sim x \to y \lor \sim y \to x)]\} \qquad D4$$

An entity is created if and only if it is not eternal (*T2*):

$$(x)(Cx \equiv \sim Ex) \qquad T2$$

Thus the entities of Whitehead's ontology are divisible into the primary dichotomy of created entities and eternal entities by means of formal properties of synonty.

15. *Physical and Mental*

Perhaps synonty is not only nonsymmetric but also asymmetric among created entities: If one created entity has already come into being for another created entity, then surely the other has not yet come into being for the one. But a prehension does not "come into being" simpliciter; instead, it comes into being "with" other prehensions in an internal process of concrescence. In particular, each one of an actual entity's prehensions is mutually sensitive with others of the actual entity's prehensions and the others are mutually sensitive with the one; although contemporaneous finite actual entities come into being separately, prehensions in the same phase come into being together. Accordingly, since synonty underlies mutual sensitivity, each prehension is synontic to some other prehension and the other prehension is synontic to it. Thus synonty is nonasymmetric among created entities (i.e.,

$$(\exists x)(\exists y)(Cx \cdot Cy \cdot x \to y \cdot y \to x)$$

where x and y are prehensions).

But synonty is asymmetric among finite actual entities. If one finite actual entity is synontic to another finite actual entity, then the other is not synontic to the one. More generally, synonty is asymmetric among finite actual entities and nexūs (*PR* 350–353). If one nexus is synontic to another nexus (and thus every actual entity in the one is synontic to every actual entity in the other), then the other is not synontic to the one (since no actual entity in the other is synontic to any actual entity in the one). Even more generally, synonty is asymmetric among finite actual entities, nexūs, and contrasts. If a contrast is synthesized by a finite actual entity, then the finite actual entity cannot be synthesized into (i.e., cannot be a component of) the contrast; if the finite actual entity is prehended by another finite actual entity and therefore the contrast can be prehended by the other finite actual entity, then the other finite actual entity cannot be synthesized into the contrast; if another contrast is synthesized by the other finite actual entity, then the one contrast can be synthesized into the other contrast but the other contrast cannot be synthesized into the one contrast. Thus synonty is asymmetric among "physical" entities (i.e., finite actual entities, nexūs, and contrasts).

However, even more generally, if a physical entity is synontic to a created entity, then the created entity is not synontic to the physical entity. A derivative created entity (i.e., a prehension, nexus, subjective form, or contrast) comes into being when the actual entity (or actual entities) from which it is derived comes into being (*PR* 33). Consequently, if a finite actual entity is synontic to another finite actual entity (or actual entities), then it is synontic to the derivative created entities derived from the other(s); but, since the other(s) is not synontic to it, the derivative created entities derived from the other(s) are not synontic to it. For example, if a finite actual entity is synontic to another finite actual entity, then it is synontic to the other's prehensions; but, since it has already come into being, none of the other's prehensions can be prehended by it. Therefore, if a nexus is synontic to a created entity (and thus every actual entity in the nexus is synontic to the created entity), then the created entity is not synontic to the nexus (since the created entity is not synontic to any actual entity in the nexus). Moreover, if a contrast is synthesized by a finite actual entity and if the finite actual entity is synontic to a created entity, then the created entity cannot be synthesized into the contrast. Thus synonty, because asymmetric among actual entities, is asymmetric between physical entities and created entities.

Although asymmetric between physical entities and created entities, synonty is nonasymmetric among prehensions and subjective forms. An actual entity's subjective forms and prehensions in the same phase, because they come into being together, are mutually sensitive; hence each prehension or subjective form is synontic to some other prehension or subjective form and the other is synontic to it. Furthermore, each eternal entity (i.e., eternal object or God) is synontic to every other entity and every other entity is synontic to it. Thus synonty is nonasymmetric among "mental" entities (i.e., prehensions, subjective forms, eternal objects, and God). ("Physical" entities can only be in an actual entity's "actual world", whereas [finite] "mental" entities constitute an actual entity as "subject"; God is appropriately a "mental" entity because he originates from his "mental pole" [by his "primordial nature"] [*PR* 54].)

Contemporaneous finite actual entities come into being separately, whereas an actual entity's subjective forms and prehensions (when in the same phase) come into being together. Thus synonty, although nonsymmetric and nonasymmetric among created entities generally, is asymmetric between physical entities and created entities and nonasymmetric among mental entities. Accordingly, I define physical entities and mental entities as follows: An entity is physical if and only if when it is synontic to a created entity the created entity is not synontic to it $(D5)$. An entity is mental if and only if it is synontic to some created entity and the created entity is synontic to it $(D6)$. Abbreviating "physical" as "P" and "mental" as "M", these definitions are abbreviated as follows:

$$(x)[Px \equiv (y)(x \to y \cdot Cy \cdot \supset \sim y \to x)] \qquad D5$$
$$(x)[Mx \equiv (\exists y)(Cy \cdot x \to y \cdot y \to x)] \qquad D6$$

An entity is physical if and only if it is not mental $(T3)$:

$$(x)(\acute{P}x \equiv \sim Mx) \qquad T3$$

Thus the entities of Whitehead's ontology are divisible into the primary dichotomy of physical entities and mental entities by means of formal properties of synony.

The primary dichotomies intersect. Some of these intersections are additional types of entity: "eternal mental" (i.e., eternal objects and God), "created mental" (i.e., prehensions and subjective forms), "mental derivative" ("finite mental") (i.e., prehensions, subjective forms, and eternal objects), "physical derivative" (i.e., nexūs and contrasts), "derivative created" (i.e., prehensions, nexūs, subjective forms, and contrasts), "finite derivative" (i.e., prehensions, nexūs, subjective forms, eternal objects, and contrasts), and "finite actual" ("created actual", "physical actual") (i.e., finite actual entities). Of immediate importance are created mental entities (i.e., prehensions and subjective forms) which I define as follows: An entity is a created mental entity if and only if it is both created and mental $(D7)$. Abbreviating "created mental" as "CM", this definition is abbreviated as follows:

$$(x)(CMx \equiv \cdot Cx \cdot Mx) \qquad D7$$

Perhaps synony is not only nonasymmetric but also symmetric among those created mental entities which are components in the concrescence of one and the same actual entity. In other words, perhaps each of an actual entity's created mental entities comes into being "with" every other. However, if one prehension can concresce into another prehension, then the other cannot concresce into the one. For a prehension in an earlier phase has already come into being when a prehension in a later phase comes into being. Accordingly, since synony underlies concrescence (and since prehensions in different phases have no other special relation which synony underlies to one another), some of an actual entity's prehensions are not synontic to others. Thus synonty is nonsymmetric among an actual entity's created mental entities.

But synonty is symmetric between an actual entity's subjective forms and its created mental entities generally. For each of its subjective forms is mutually sensitive with every other of its subjective forms and all of its prehensions. Since synonty underlies mutual sensitivity, each of its subjective forms is synontic to every other of its subjective forms, each of its subjective forms is synontic to all of its prehensions, and each of its prehensions is synontic to all of its subjective forms.

Thus each of an actual entity's created mental entities is "compresent" with all. For each comes into being "with" some created mental entity that comes into being "with" all. In particular, when one of its prehensions cannot concresce into another, the one is nonetheless mutually sensitive with some subjective form mutually sensitive with the other. Since synonty underlies mutual sensitivity, each of an actual entity's created mental entities is "mediately" synontic to (i.e., "compresent" with) all.

But none of an actual entity's created mental entities is compresent with any of any other actual entity's created mental entities. Since a past actual entity has already come into being, its subjective forms can only be "re-enacted"; there is no *mutual* sensitivity. Since a contemporary actual entity comes into being in a "unison of becoming" that is nonetheless separate, it cannot be prehended at all; thus there is no sensitivity at all. Hence an actual entity's subjective forms and prehensions (when in the same phase) are mutually sensitive only with one another. Since synonty underlies mutual sensitivity, an actual entity's created mental entities are therefore compresent only with one another.

I define the relation of compresence as follows: An entity is compresent with an entity if and only if they are created mental entities synontic to some created mental entity synontic to them (*D8*). Abbreviating "*x* is compresent with *y*" as "*x*Δ*y*" (where the "Δ" pictures the convergence of many prehensions to one actual entity), this definition is abbreviated as follows:

$$x \, \Delta \, y \equiv [CMx \cdot CMy \cdot (\exists z)(CMz \cdot x \to z \cdot z \to x \cdot y \to z \cdot z \to y)] \qquad D8$$

Compresence, because reflexive, symmetric, and transitive, is an equivalence relation. (A relation *Rxy* is transitive when

$$(x)(y)(z)(Rxy \cdot Ryz \cdot \supset Rxz).)$$

Each of an actual entity's created mental entities is compresent with itself (since it is mutually sensitive with some subjective form) (reflexiveness). If one of its created mental entities is compresent with another, then the other is compresent with the one (since both are mutually sensitive with some subjective form) (symmetry). If one of its created mental entities is compresent with a second, and the second with a third, then the one is compresent with the third (since each of its subjective forms is mutually sensitive with every other of its created mental entities) (transitivity).

Created mental entities are decomposable by means of compresence into "clusters". (An equivalence relation decomposes its field into mutually exclusive and jointly exhaustive equivalence classes.) For each actual entity's prehensions and subjective forms, because compresent to one another but not to any other actual entity's prehensions and subjective forms, "cluster" together. Accordingly, I define the entities in an arbitrary cluster as follows: (For the sake of clarity, I define the entities in an arbitrary cluster rather than clustered entities generally [i.e., the "class" of clusters], and state the definition in two stages.) Any two entities in the cluster are compresent ($D9a$). If an entity is compresent with any entity in the cluster, then it is itself in the cluster ($D9b$). Abbreviating "an arbitrary cluster" as "CL_i", this definition is abbreviated as follows:

$$(x)(y)(CL_i x \cdot CL_i y \cdot \supset x \Delta y) \qquad\qquad D9a$$
$$(x)(y)(x \Delta y \cdot CL_i y \cdot \supset CL_i x) \qquad\qquad D9b$$

An actual entity comes into being by means of a process involving the "concrescence" of its prehensions. It is not just the "class" of its prehensions. Thus I do not use the "method of logical construction" to define actual entities. In particular, I do not use the equivalence relation of compresence to "construct" actual entities as equivalence classes of created mental entities. Instead, I use the equivalence relation of compresence to "distinguish" the *components* of one actual entity (i.e., the created mental entities which concresce into that actual entity) from the components of every other actual entity. The apparatus of logic has alternative uses appropriate to alternative metaphysics.

16. *Actual and Derivative*

Synonty is, in a very general sense, an "ordering" relation among created entities. Since created entities are interwoven by the special relations which synonty underlies, synonty "orders" ("arranges") each created entity with respect to every other. But, in a sense, *any* relation "orders" its field (cf. the representation of a relation by an "arrow diagram", and the definition of the extension of a relation as a class of "ordered pairs"): Because one relatum of a relation either has or does not have the relation to another relatum (and the other either does or does not have the relation to the one), each relatum has a "position" with respect to every other. However, synonty not only "positions" created entities but also gives them "direction" and makes them "sequential". For there is a "creative *advance*" of actual entities (and, therefore, derivatively, of created entities generally). Thus synonty is an "ordering" relation among created entities not only by "positioning" them but also by "directioning" and "sequencing" them.

The most familiar ordering relation is a "serial relation": a relation which is irreflexive, asymmetric, transitive, and connected (e.g., the relation "is greater than" among the integers). But synonty is not connected among created entities. (A relation Rxy is connected when, for each x and y in its field,

$$x \neq y \supset \cdot Rxy \lor Ryx;$$

a relation Rxy is disconnected when, for each x and y in its field,

$$x \neq y \supset \cdot {\sim}Rxy \cdot {\sim}Ryx.)$$

In particular, contemporaneous finite actual entities do not prehend one another, and, therefore, each finite actual entity is not synontic to some finite actual entities not synontic to it. Thus synonty is not a serial relation among created entities (*PR* 52).

But a relation which is irreflexive, asymmetric, transitive, and not connected is still an ordering relation, namely, a "strict partial ordering" (e.g., the relation "is a proper subclass of" among classes). However, synonty is not asymmetric among created entities. In particular, prehensions in the same phase are mutually sensitive, and, therefore, each prehension is synontic to some prehensions synontic to it. Thus synonty is not a strict partial ordering among created entities. Moreover, synonty is not transitive among created entities. Since each prehension is synontic to some other prehension synontic to it, if synonty were transitive, it would be synontic to itself; but no prehension is synontic to itself. (A relation which is irreflexive and nonasymmetric cannot be transitive.) Thus synonty, although irreflexive, is not connected, not asymmetric, and not transitive among created entities. In what sense, then, is it an "ordering relation"?

Although not connected, synonty is what I term "mediately connected" among created entities: For any two different created entities, one is synontic to some created entity synontic to the other, or, the other is synontic to some created entity synontic to the one, or, both are synontic to some created entity, or, some created entity is synontic to both. (A relation Rxy is mediately connected when the second power of the relation $Rxy \lor Ryx$ is connected; a relation S^2xy is the second power of the relation Sxy when

$$(x)(y)[S^2xy \equiv (\exists z)(Sxz \cdot Szy)];$$

thus Rxy is mediately connected when, for each x and y in its field,

$$x \neq y \supset (\exists z)(Rxz \cdot Rzy \cdot \lor \cdot Ryz \cdot Rzx \cdot \lor \cdot Rxz \cdot Ryz \cdot \lor \cdot Rzx \cdot Rzy).)$$

In particular, synonty, although not connected among the entities in a cluster, is mediately connected among them (because they are created mental entities synontic to some created mental entity synontic to them). Also, synonty, although not connected among finite actual entities, is mediately connected among them (because contemporaneous finite actual entities are synontic to some finite actual entity in their future [and some finite actual entity in their past is synontic to them]). Thus synonty, even though not connected, "positions" created entities very closely together in an unpartitioned network. (In general, a relation "positions" entities in an unpartitioned network when it is what I term "quasi-connected"; a relation Rxy is quasi-connected when the ancestral of the relation $Rxy \lor Ryx$ is connected; in the gamut of quasi-connected relations, connected relations and mediately connected relations "position" their relata most "closely".)

Although not asymmetric among created entities, synonty is asymmetric among physical entities. Moreover, synonty is transitive among finite actual entities. If one finite actual entity is prehended by a second, and the second by a third, then the first is prehended by the third. (Hence actual worlds are "cumulative"; the universe is "historical".) More generally, synonty is transitive among finite actual entities and nexūs. If one nexus is synontic to a second (and thus every actual entity in the first is synontic to every actual entity in the second), and if the second is synontic to a third (and thus every actual entity in the second is synontic to every actual entity in the third), then the first is synontic to the third (since every actual entity in the first is therefore synontic to every actual entity in the third). Even more generally, synonty is transitive among finite actual entities, nexūs, and contrasts. If one contrast is synontic to a second (because the actual entity which synthesizes the first is synontic to the actual entity which synthesizes the second), and if the second is synontic to a third (because the actual entity which synthesizes the second is synontic to the actual entity which synthesizes the third), then the first is synontic to the third (because the actual entity which synthesizes the first is synontic to the actual entity which synthesizes the third). (Thus the creative advance of physical entities generally is derivative from the creative advance of actual entities.) Therefore, even though not a strict partial ordering of created entities generally, synonty, because irreflexive, asymmetric, and transitive among physical entities, is a strict partial ordering of physical entities.

Although asymmetric only among physical entities and not among created entities generally, synonty is what I term "derivatively asymmetric" among created entities, and, therefore, gives them "direction". For it is asymmetric between physical entities and created entities. Thus it is derivatively asymmetric among created entities in that it is asymmetric among created entities when at least one of its relata is a physical entity (i.e., for any two created entities x and y,

$$x \rightarrow y \cdot (Px \lor Py) \cdot \supset \sim y \rightarrow x \,).$$

Although not transitive among created entities generally, synonty is what I term "strictly transitive" among created entities other than subjective forms (i.e., physical entities and prehensions). (A relation Rxy is transitive when

$$(x)(y)(z)(Rxy \cdot Ryz \cdot \supset Rxz);$$

a relation Rxy is *strictly* transitive when

$$(x)(y)(z)(Rxy \cdot Ryz \cdot x \neq z \cdot \supset Rxz);$$

thus a strictly transitive relation is transitive between *different* entities [cf. antisymmetry].) In particular, synonty, although transitive among prehensions in different phases, is only strictly transitive among prehensions in the same phase: If one prehension is mutually sensitive with a second, and the second with a third, then the first is mutually sensitive with the third only when they are *different* prehensions (since each prehension is mutually sensitive with every *other* prehension in the same phase, and no prehension is mutually sensitive with itself). But synonty is not strictly transitive among created mental entities generally: If one prehension can concresce into another prehension, then—since the other is mutually sensitive with a subjective form mutually sensitive with the one—if synonty were strictly transitive among created mental entities generally, the other would be synontic to the one.

The subjective forms in a cluster are mutually sensitive, whereas the prehensions are divisible into the "phases" in which they come into being. In particular, prehensions in the same phase of becoming are mutually sensitive, and, a prehension in an earlier phase can concresce into a prehension in a later phase, but the prehension in the later phase cannot concresce into the prehension in the earlier phase. Therefore, any two prehensions in the same phase are synontic to each other, and, if a prehension is synontic to a prehension in the phase and the prehension in the phase is synontic to it, then it is itself in the phase. Thus the relation "x is synontic to y and y is synontic to x" decomposes prehensions into phases. (However, this relation is not reflexive, symmetric, and transitive, but rather is irreflexive, symmetric, and strictly transitive; therefore, it is not an equivalence relation, but rather what I term a "strict equivalence relation" [another example of a strict equivalence relation being the relation of congruence restricted to *different* geometrical figures].) Consequently, one phase is earlier than another phase if and only if a prehension in the one is synontic to a prehension in the other. Thus synonty defines a serial ordering of phases of prehensions.

Although not strictly transitive among created entities, synonty is what I term "derivatively transitive" among them, and, therefore, makes them "sequential". In particular, it is derivatively transitive among them in that it is transitive among them when at least one of its relata is a physical entity (i.e., for any three created entities x, y, and z,

$$x \rightarrow y \cdot y \rightarrow z \cdot (Px \lor Py \lor Pz) \cdot \supset x \rightarrow z).$$

For example, if one prehension is synontic to an actual entity, and the actual entity is synontic to another prehension (and thus the one is not compresent with the other), then the one is synontic to the other (because the actual entity which concresces from the one is prehended by the actual entity which concresces from the other). Thus the ordering of created entities is derived from the ordering of physical entities.

A serial relation is irreflexive, asymmetric, transitive, and connected. Because connected, it "positions" its relata closely together; because asymmetric, it gives them "direction"; because transitive, it makes them "sequential". In contrast, synonty, although irreflexive, is not asymmetric, not transitive, and not connected among created entities; nonetheless, it is derivatively asymmetric, derivatively transitive, and mediately connected among them. Because mediately connected, it "positions" them closely together; because derivatively asymmetric, it gives them "direction"; because derivatively transitive, it makes them "sequential". However, the "positioning" is sometimes not proximate, the "directioning" is not uniform, and the "sequencing" is not linear. Therefore, although not a serial relation among created entities, synonty is a generalized analogue of a serial relation among them.

Synonty is derivatively asymmetric and derivatively transitive among created entities in that it is asymmetric and transitive among them when at least one of its relata is a physical entity. Consequently, each physical entity is either an "upper bound" or what I term a "partial lower bound" to the entities in a cluster. (Analogously, an upper bound b to a class S of entities in the field of the serial relation $x < y$ is such that

$$(x)[Sx \supset (x < b \lor x = b)];$$

what I term a "partial lower bound" b to a class S of entities in the field of the strict partial ordering $x < y$ is such that

$$(x)[Sx \supset (b < x \cdot \lor \cdot x = b \cdot \lor \cdot {\sim}b < x \cdot {\sim}x < b)].)$$

If an entity is a cluster is synontic to a physical entity, then, since each entity in the cluster is comprement with every entity in the cluster, and since synonty is derivatively transitive, every entity in the cluster is synontic to the physical entity. Thus the physical entity is an "upper bound" to the entities in the cluster. If a physical entity is synontic to an entity in a cluster, then, for each other entity in the cluster, either the physical entity is synontic to the entity or it is not synontic to the entity and the entity is not synontic to it. (In particular, when a contrast is synthesized by an actual entity, it is synontic to some of the actual entity's prehensions but not to others [e.g., the actual entity's simple physical feelings] .) Thus the physical entity is a "partial lower bound" to the entities in the cluster. (Hence a physical entity p is either an "upper bound" or a "partial lower bound" to a cluster CL_i in that either

$$(x)(CL_i x \supset x \to p)$$

or

$$(x)[CL_i x \supset (p \to x \cdot \vee \cdot \sim p \to x \cdot \sim x \to p)].)$$

A finite actual entity is a "least upper bound" to the cluster of prehensions and subjective forms which concresce into it. (Analogously, a least upper bound b to a class S of entities in the field of the serial relation $x < y$ is an upper bound to S such that, for any other upper bound b' to S, $b < b'$.) For it is the "first" physical entity to come into being for which they have already come into being. When they can be prehended by an actual entity, it can also be prehended by that actual entity. When they are synontic to a nexus (and thus can be prehended by every actual entity in the nexus), it is synontic to the nexus (since it can be prehended by every actual entity in the nexus). When they can be synthesized into a contrast (and thus can be prehended by the actual entity which synthesizes the contrast), it can be synthesized into the contrast (since it can be prehended by the actual entity which synthesizes the contrast). In short, if the entities in a cluster are synontic to a physical entity other than the finite actual entity into which they concresce, then the finite actual entity into which they concresce is also synontic to the physical entity.

A finite actual entity is not just the "class" of its prehensions and subjective forms, but comes into being through the concrescence of its prehensions and subjective forms, and thus is synontic to any other physical entity to which its prehensions and subjective forms are synontic. Hence a finite actual entity is the "least upper bound" of its prehensions and subjective forms. Accordingly, I define finite actual entities as follows: An entity is a finite actual entity if and only if it is a physical entity to which some created mental entity is synontic and it is synontic to any other physical entity to which the created mental entity is synontic ($D10$). Abbreviating "finite actual" as "A", this definition is abbreviated as follows:

$$(x)\{Ax \equiv \cdot Px \cdot (\exists y)[CMy \cdot y \to x \cdot (z)(Pz \cdot x \neq z \cdot y \to z \cdot \supset x \to z)]\}$$
$$D10$$

Finite actual entities are the "least upper bounds" of clusters, whereas nexūs and contrasts are not. If a created mental entity is synontic to a nexus, then it is synontic to some other physical entity to which the nexus is not synontic, for example, some actual entity in the nexus. If a created mental entity is synontic to a contrast, then it is synontic to some physical entity to which the contrast is not synontic, namely, the actual entity into which it concresces. Thus only finite actual entities satisfy their definition.

According to Whitehead, finite actual entities are divisible into six types of "locus" by means of the relation of prehension (*PR* 486–488). Since synonty underlies prehension, these types of locus are definable by means of formal properties of synonty. Thus the hierarchy of types of entity defined by means of synonty encompasses definitions expressly stated in *Process and Reality*.

The finite actual entities prehended by (i.e., in the actual world of) a finite actual entity M comprise the "causal past" of M. Thus a finite actual entity is in the causal past of M if and only if it is synontic to M. The finite actual entities which prehend M (i.e., which have M in their actual worlds) comprise the "causal future" of M. Thus a finite actual entity is in the causal future of M if and only if M is synontic to it. The finite actual entities which neither prehend M nor are prehended by M comprise the "contemporaries" of M. Thus a finite actual entity is among the contemporaries of M if and only if it is not synontic to M and M is not synontic to it. In general, any finite actual entity other than M is either in the causal past of M or in the causal future of M or among the contemporaries of M. In short, three types of locus of finite actual entities are the causal past of a finite actual entity, the causal future of a finite actual entity, and the contemporaries of a finite actual entity.

Any two finite actual entities among the contemporaries of a finite actual entity need not be contemporaries of one another. (Analogously, according to the special theory of relativity, simultaneity is "relative".) Therefore, the relation of "contemporaneity" (i.e., x is not prehended by y and y is not prehended by x), although reflexive and symmetric among finite actual entities, is not transitive among them. Thus the relation "x is not synontic to y and y is not synontic to x" is reflexive, symmetric, and not transitive among finite actual entities.

Just as created mental entities are decomposable by means of compresence into clusters, so finite actual entities are decomposable by means of contemporaneity into "durations" (the fourth type of locus). However, compresence is an equivalence relation and clusters are equivalence classes, whereas contemporaneity is a "similarity relation" and durations are "similarity circles". For contemporaneity is not transitive among finite actual entities. (An equivalence relation is reflexive, symmetric, and transitive, whereas a similarity relation is reflexive and symmetric; an equivalence class S defined by the equivalence relation Rxy is such that

$$(x)(y)(Sx \cdot Sy \cdot \supset Rxy)$$

and

$$(x)[(\exists y)(Sy \cdot Rxy) \supset Sx],$$

whereas a similarity circle S defined by the similarity relation Rxy is such that

$$(x)(y)(Sx \cdot Sy \cdot \supset Rxy)$$

and

$$(x)[(y)(Sy \supset Rxy) \supset Sx];$$

consequently, if an entity has the equivalence relation to *any* entity in the equivalence class, then, because equivalence relations are transitive, it is itself in the equivalence class, whereas, because similarity relations need not be transitive, only when an entity has the similarity relation to *every* entity in the similarity circle is it itself in the similarity circle.) [1]

Any two finite actual entities in a particular duration are contemporaneous. For the finite actual entities in the same duration are in a "unison of becoming" (*PR* 487). Thus any two finite actual entities in a particular duration are not synontic to each other.

Any finite actual entity not in a particular duration is not contemporaneous with some of the finite actual entities in the duration. In other words, any finite actual entity not in a particular duration either prehends or is prehended by some of the finite actual entities in the duration. Nonetheless, a finite actual entity not in a particular duration may be contemporaneous with some other of the finite actual entities in the duration: Even though a finite actual entity is contemporaneous with a finite actual entity in a particular duration, it need not be contemporaneous with every finite actual entity in the duration, for contemporaneity is not transitive. Thus a finite actual entity not in a particular duration is synontic to some finite actual entity in the duration or some finite actual entity in the duration is synontic to it.

A duration is an "old-fashioned 'present state of the world'" (*PR* 487), since the finite actual entities in a particular duration are all contemporaries. Accordingly, Whitehead defines the entities in a particular duration as follows (*PR* 487): Any two finite actual entities in the duration are contemporaneous (cf. *D11a*). If a finite actual entity is contemporaneous with every finite actual entity in the duration, then it is itself in the duration (cf. *D11b*). Therefore, since synonty underlies prehension, I define the entities in an arbitrary duration by means of synonty as follows: Any two finite actual entities in the duration are not synontic to each other (*D11a*). If a finite actual entity is not synontic to any finite actual entity in the duration and no finite actual entity in the duration is synontic to it, then it is itself in the duration (*D11b*). Abbreviating "an arbitrary duration" as "DR_i", this definition is abbreviated as follows:

$$(x)(y)(DR_i x \cdot DR_i y \cdot \supset \cdot Ax \cdot Ay \cdot \sim x \to y \cdot \sim y \to x) \qquad D11a$$
$$(x)[(y)(DR_i y \supset \cdot Ax \cdot Ay \cdot \sim x \to y \cdot \sim y \to x) \supset DR_i x] \qquad D11b$$

Just as the relation "x is not prehended by y and y is not prehended by x" is a similarity relation which decomposes finite actual entities into durations, so the relation "x is prehended by y or y is prehended by x" is what I term a "strict similarity relation" which decomposes finite actual entities into what I term "world lines" (a type of locus not defined by Whitehead). (A strict similarity relation is irreflexive and symmetric.) Thus any two different finite actual entities in a particular world line are such that one prehends the other, and, if a finite actual entity either prehends or is prehended by every other finite actual entity in the world line, then it is itself in the world line. For example, an "enduring object", which, according to Whitehead, is a linear series of finite actual entities (*PR* 51–52), is a segment of a world line. (However, the world lines defined by means of synonty are only analogues of the world lines of the special theory of relativity.)

The finite actual entities prehended by any of the finite actual entities in a duration D comprise the "past" of D. Thus a finite actual entity is in the past of D if and only if it is synontic to some finite actual entity in D. The finite actual entities which prehend any of the finite actual entities in D comprise the "future" of D. Thus a finite actual entity is in the future of D if and only if some finite actual entity in D is synontic to it. In general, any finite actual entity is either in D or in the past of D or in the future of D. In short, two types of locus of finite actual entities are the past of a duration and the future of a duration. Therefore, the six types of locus of finite actual entities defined in *Process and Reality* by means of prehension—the causal past of a finite actual entity, the causal future of a

finite actual entity, the contemporaries of a finite actual entity, durations, the past of a duration, and the future of a duration—are definable by means of formal properties of synonty.

Whereas each of an actual entity's prehensions is in just one
phase of concrescence, each finite actual entity is in many durations
(*PR* 487–488). Accordingly, there are durations such that some finite actual entity in one is synontic to some finite actual entity in the
other and some finite actual entity in the other is synontic to some
finite actual entity in the one. Therefore, in contrast to the phases
of concrescence, durations are not serially ordered. Nonetheless, synonty defines a strict partial ordering of durations: One duration is
"earlier" than another duration when they are different and no finite
actual entity in the other is synontic to any finite actual entity in the
one.

Actual entities are the "final realities", whereas entities of the
other basic types are "derived" from them. Accordingly, I define derivative entities (i.e., prehensions, nexūs, subjective forms, eternal
objects, and contrasts) as follows: An entity is derivative if and only
if it is finite but not a finite actual entity (*D12*). Abbreviating "derivative" as "*D*", this definition is abbreviated as follows:

$$(x)(Dx \equiv \cdot Fx \cdot \sim Ax) \qquad\qquad D12$$

Thus the entities of Whitehead's ontology are divisible into the primary dichotomy of derivative entities and (finite or infinite) actual
entities.

17. The Categories of Existence

According to Whitehead, God is an instance, albeit variant (because
"primordial"), of an actual entity. Thus the actual entities are the
finite actual entities together with the infinite entities. Accordingly,
I define actual entities as follows: An entity is an actual entity if
and only if it is either a finite actual entity or an infinite entity
(*D13*). Abbreviating "actual entity" as "*AE*", this definition is abbreviated as follows:

$$(x)(AEx \equiv \cdot Ax \lor Ix) \qquad\qquad D13$$

God is synontic to every entity and every entity is synontic to
him, whereas each eternal object is synontic to every other entity

and every other entity is synontic to it. For God can prehend himself, whereas an eternal object cannot be a component of itself. Accordingly, I define eternal objects as follows: An entity is an eternal object if and only if it is eternal and not synontic to itself (*D14*). Abbreviating "eternal object" as "*EO*", this definition is abbreviated as follows:

$$(x)(EOx \equiv \cdot Ex \cdot \sim x \to x) \qquad D14$$

A subjective form in a cluster is mutually sensitive with every other subjective form in the cluster and with every prehension in the cluster, whereas a prehension in the cluster cannot concresce into or be concresced into by some other prehensions in the cluster. Accordingly, I define subjective forms and prehensions as follows: An entity is a subjective form if and only if it is a created mental entity such that it is synontic to every other entity with which it is comprevent and every other entity with which it is comprevent is synontic to it (*D15*). An entity is a prehension if and only if it is a created mental entity such that it is not synontic to some other entity with which it is comprevent or some other entity with which it is comprevent is not synontic to it (*D16*). Abbreviating "subjective form" as "*SF*" and "prehension" as "*PR*", these definitions are abbreviated as follows:

$$(x)[SFx \equiv \cdot CMx \cdot (y)(x \neq y \cdot x \bigtriangleup y \cdot \supset \cdot x \to y \cdot y \to x)] \qquad D15$$
$$(x)\{PRx \equiv \cdot CMx \cdot (\exists y)[x \neq y \cdot x \bigtriangleup y \cdot (\sim x \to y \vee \sim y \to x)]\} \qquad D16$$

Consequently, if an entity is a created mental entity, then it is a subjective form if and only if it is not a prehension (*T4*):

$$(x)(CMx \supset \cdot SFx \equiv \sim PRx) \qquad T4$$

A contrast is not merely an "ordered pair" of entities but instead is a novel entity produced through the synethesis of the entities contrasted. When an actual entity produces an integral feeling of a contrast and thereby synthesizes the contrast, the contrast is synontic to some of the actual entity's prehensions (e.g., the integral feeling) but not to others (e.g., the actual entity's simple physical feelings). Accordingly, I define contrasts as follows: An entity is a contrast if and only if it is a physical entity synontic to some created mental entity comprevent with some created mental entity to which it is not synontic (*D17*). Abbreviating "contrast" as "*CN*", this definition is abbreviated as follows:

$$(x)[CNx \equiv \cdot Px \cdot (\exists y)(\exists z)(y \Delta z \cdot x \to y \cdot \sim x \to z)] \qquad D17$$

A cluster, a phase, or a duration is not a "proper" entity but merely a multiplicity of entities, whereas a nexus is not merely a multiplicity of finite actual entities but is itself a novel entity produced by means of those finite actual entities' prehensions of one another. Thus I do not define the actual entities in a particular nexus but rather nexūs themselves. For simplicity, I define nexūs as follows: An entity is a nexus if and only if it is a physical entity but neither a finite actual entity nor a contrast (*D18*). Abbreviating "nexus" as "*NX*", this definition is abbreviated as follows:

$$(x)(NXx \equiv \cdot Px \cdot \sim Ax \cdot \sim CNx) \qquad D18$$

In summary, Whitehead's "Categories of Existence"—actual entities, eternal objects, subjective forms, prehensions, contrasts, and nexūs—are definable by means of formal properties of the universal relation of synonty.

Notes

Notes for Preface

1. *Process and Reality: An Essay in Cosmology* (New York, 1929).

2. The most important of Whitehead's earlier writings are *A Treatise on Universal Algebra* (Cambridge, 1898), *Principia Mathematica* (with Bertrand Russell) (Cambridge, 1910–13), *An Enquiry Concerning the Principles of Natural Knowledge* (Cambridge, 1919), *The Concept of Nature* (Cambridge, 1920), and *The Principle of Relativity* (Cambridge, 1922).

The most important of his later writings are *Science and the Modern World* (New York, 1925), *Process and Reality* (New York, 1929), and *Adventures of Ideas* (New York, 1933).

The standard bibliography of his writings is contained in *The Philosophy of Alfred North Whitehead*, ed. P. A. Schilpp, 2d ed. (New York, 1951), pp. 751–779.

For an interesting survey of the development of his thought see Victor Lowe, *Understanding Whitehead* (Baltimore, 1962), pp. 117–296.

For interpretations of *Process and Reality* see William A. Christian, *An Interpretation of Whitehead's Metaphysics* (New Haven, 1959); Ivor Leclerc, *Whitehead's Metaphysics: An Introductory Exposition* (London, 1958); and Donald W. Sherburne, *A Whiteheadian Aesthetic: Some Implications of Whitehead's Metaphysical Speculation* (New Haven, 1961), pp. 3–88.

For useful bibliographies of writings about Whitehead see Walter Stokes, "A Select and Annotated Bibliography of Alfred North Whitehead", *Modern Schoolman*, 39 (1962): 135–151, and Paul F. Schmidt, *Perception and Cosmology in Whitehead's Philosophy* (New Brunswick, 1967), pp. 181–188.

Notes for Chapter 1

1. There are, unfortunately, three different paginations of *Process and Reality* (and no standard edition)—namely, (1) that of the Macmillan hardback (New York, 1929) and the Harper & Row paperback (New York, 1960), (2) that of the English hardback (Cambridge, 1929), and (3) that of the Macmillan paperback (New York, 1969). Parenthetical references of the above form are to (1).

2. For an illustration of the incomprehension with which *Process and Reality*

was greeted upon its publication see L. Susan Stebbing's "Critical Notice" in *Mind*, 39 (1930): 466–475. But more recent studies—in particular, Christian's *An Interpretation of Whitehead's Metaphysics*—have eased the task of interpretation.

3. In "The Influence of Logic and Mathematics on Whitehead", *Journal of the History of Ideas*, 20 (1959): 420–430, David Harrah argues that the Whitehead of *Process and Reality* is still the Whitehead of *Principia Mathematica*, because Whitehead always construed the "activity" of "mathematizing" in a broad sense rather than a narrow, namely, as concerned with relations in general rather than merely with deduction, and as creative rather than merely rigorous (pp. 421–422).

4. Although Christian includes, in *An Interpretation of Whitehead's Metaphysics*, a section entitled "examples of eternal objects" (pp. 202–203), I am unable to find any discussion of examples of actual entities (other than God) (but see the section entitled "The question of evidence" [pp. 168–172]).

5. Since my aim is merely to define Whitehead's categories of existence and not to define the types of entity falling under each category, I shall discuss only some of the many differences between finite actual entities and God. For a thorough discussion of the many problems raised by Whitehead's categorization of God as an actual entity, see Christian's *Interpretation*, pp. 283–413.

6. In *Adventures of Ideas* (New York: The New American Library, 1955), Whitehead states that our experience of our own immediate past is an example of nonsensuous (conscious) perception (pp. 182–185). But his purpose is not to show that we can consciously perceive an individual actual entity but rather to show that conscious perception can be nonsensuous as well as sensuous. Therefore, his purpose is achieved whether his example is classified as a simple physical feeling or as a transmuted physical feeling.

7. For example, Rudolf Carnap, *Introduction to Symbolic Logic and Its Applications*, trans. William H. Meyer and John Wilkinson (New York, 1958), pp. 114–156.

8. In his *Introduction to Symbolic Logic*, Carnap discusses equivalence relations (and the definition of cardinal numbers) (pp. 136–141) but not similarity relations, even though, in his *The Logical Structure of the World*, trans. Rolf A. George (London, 1967), he discusses similarity relations (and the definition of colors) (pp. 22, 110–120, 125–133, 163–164, 178–186).

9. Although not mentioned by Carnap in his discussion of ordering relations (*Introduction*, pp. 122–125), a relation which is irreflexive, asymmetric, and transitive (but which need not be connected) is termed by Patrick Suppes, *Introduction to Logic* (Princeton, 1957), a "strict partial ordering" (p. 222).

10. In his *From a Logical Point of View*, 2d ed. (New York and Evanston, 1963), pp. 1–19.

11. *Critique of Pure Reason*, trans. Norman Kemp Smith (London, 1958), pp. 104–119 (B91–B116).

12. Bertrand Russell, in the Preface to his *Our Knowledge of the External World* (London, 1914), states that he owes to Whitehead "the whole conception of the world of physics as a *construction* rather than an *inference*". See also his *The Analysis of Matter* (London, 1927), Chapter 28 ("The Construction of Points"), where he construes Whitehead's definition of points as a paradigm of logical construction (pp. 290–292).

13. In an attempt to explicate Whitehead's metaphysics using set theory, Lucio Chiaraviglio, in his "Extension and Abstraction", *Process and Divinity: Philosophical Essays Presented to Charles Hartshorne*, ed. William L. Reese and Eugene Freeman (LaSalle, Ill., 1964), pp. 205–216, defines actual entities as the equivalence subsets of the set of prehensions with respect to the equivalence relation "has the same subject as" (p. 206).

14. In addition to the "classic" attempt to dispense with eternal objects— Everett W. Hall's "Of What Use Are Whitehead's Eternal Objects", *Journal of Philosophy*, 27 (1930): 29–44—the construction of eternal objects as classes ("sets") is attempted by Chiaraviglio in "Whitehead's Theory of Prehensions", *Alfred North Whitehead: Essays on His Philosophy*, ed. George L. Kline (Englewood Cliffs, N. J., 1963), pp. 81–92. Now eternal objects, which are modeled after Plato's forms, function ("participate") as "lures for feeling" in the concrescence of actual entities (*PR* 63, 133). But can a "class" function as a "final cause"?

Notes for Chapter 2

1. *Alfred North Whitehead: An Anthology*, ed. F. S. C. Northrop and Mason W. Gross (New York, 1961), pp. 11–12, 32–34, 60, 81–82.

2. (New York: The New American Library, 1948), pp. 157–173.

3. For a lucid summary of Whitehead's theory of concrescence see Sherburne's "Concrescence", the third chapter of his *A Whiteheadian Aesthetic*, pp. 41–71.

4. Christian, in his *Interpretation*, although puzzled about how phases can be in a succession, maintains that the succession of phases is not a temporal succession (pp. 80–81). But I contend that the succession of actual entities and the succession of phases of prehensions are both successions of becomings (and thus are united in the succession of created entities [see my Section 16]). Are our two views incompatible? An actual entity, when its process of concrescence is complete, "perishes" (but is "objectively immortal" [i.e., is prehended by future actual entities]) (*PR* 94); hence its prehensions, although they come into being in a succession of phases, only perish when it perishes. Now Whitehead links time with perishing (*PR* 43, 196). Thus the temporal succession is not merely a succession of becomings but a succession of becomings and perishings.

5. In *A Whiteheadian Aesthetic*, Sherburne maintains that art objects are propositions (pp. 98–133). But he misinterprets Whitehead's theory of propositions, for he thinks that a proposition "preserves the indeterminateness of an eternal object" because it "abstracts from the fully determinate actual entities which are the datum of the component physical feeling" (pp. 103–104). However, according to Whitehead, even though a propositional feeling is not a feeling of the "real role in actuality" of the actual entity (or nexus) which is the "subject" of the proposition felt, nonetheless it contains a "physical indication" of that actual entity (or nexus) (*PR* 394).

6. See his *An Enquiry Concerning the Principles of Natural Knowledge*, pp. 68–69.

7. For a more detailed account of Whitehead's theory of perception see

Schmidt's *Perception and Cosmology in Whitehead's Philosophy*, pp. 99–168. But Schmidt's account is more adequate to Part II of *Process and Reality* than to Part IV; in particular, he summarizes but does not adequately interpret Whitehead's theory of "projection" (pp. 136–144).

8. Op. cit. and (Ann Arbor, 1957).

9. Adolf Grünbaum, in his influential *Philosophical Problems of Space and Time* (New York, 1963), criticizes "Whitehead's theory of relativity" without comprehending this development in Whitehead's views (pp. 344–345, 425–428). In particular, he criticizes "Whitehead's attempt to ground the concept of distant simultaneity of physical theory on the sensed coincidences experienced by sentient observers" (p. 344), and argues, in opposition, that the temporal relations between events are grounded on a "physical relation of causal connectibility" (p. 347). But Whitehead, by replacing the concept of cogredience by the concept of prehension, is, in effect, replacing a concept of "sensed coincidences" by a concept of "causal connectibility". Accordingly, Grünbaum's definition of "topological simultaneity" (two events are topologically simultaneous just in case neither is causally connectible with the other) (p. 348) is the equivalent of Whitehead's definition of contemporaneity.

Note for Chapter 3

1. For a fuller account of the logic of similarity circles see Carnap, *The Logical Structure of the World*, pp. 110–120. Also see my "The Logic of Simultaneity", *The Journal of Philosophy*, vol. 66, no. 11 (5 June 1969): 340–350.

Index